SEÁN LEMASS

SEÁN LEMASS

BRIAN FARRELL

GILL AND MACMILLAN

Published in Ireland by
Gill and Macmillan Ltd
Goldenbridge
Dublin 8
with associated companies in
Auckland, Delhi, Gaborone, Hamburg, Harare,
Hong Kong, Johannesburg, Kuala Lumpur, Lagos, London,
Manzini, Melbourne, Mexico City, Nairobi,
New York, Singapore, Tokyo
© Brian Farrell 1983, 1991
0 7171 1885 1
First published 1983 as part of
the Gill's Irish Lives series
Print origination by
Galaxy Reproductions Ltd, Dublin
Printed by
Billings Ltd, Worcester

Contents

Preface

This brief biography attempts to sketch some of the major themes in the long public career of Seán Lemass. It has grown from an original essay on his period as Taoiseach and I am grateful to Dermot Ryan for access to his unique collection of recorded Lemass interviews in the preparation of *Chairman or Chief*. The present work is grounded in an examination of available public records and papers. It owes much to a number of interviews with Mr Lemass, members of his family and some of those most closely associated with him in politics and in government. As far as possible I have tried to let Lemass speak for himself and have drawn constantly on the invaluable Lemass interviews by Michael Mills in the *Irish Press*; the many quotations are intended to convey an impression of the man in his own words.

Inevitably many important events are passed over or, at best, barely touched upon; in particular, his unique contribution to the development of the semi-state sector requires much fuller treatment. Equally the private man rarely emerges from behind the public figure. What is offered is an interim and necessarily incomplete political biography. A fuller account must await the opening of further archival material and the unlocking of more personal memories.

I should like to acknowledge the co-operation and assistance of members of the Lemass family, of his political colleagues and associates, of civil servants who served with him, of my own colleagues and students in the Department of Ethics and Politics, University College, Dublin and of the helpful staffs in the National Library, State Paper and Public Record Offices, the Library and Archives Department of University College, Dublin, the libraries of the *Irish Press*, Institute of Public

Administration and RTE. I am especially grateful to Dr Maurice Moynihan for his courtesy and encouragement, and for his kindness in reading the typescript of this biography. Particular thanks are due to Geraldine Meyler who translated poor handwriting into impeccable typing, to my son, David Farrell, for his assistance in combing some of the Dáil debates, and to Fergal Tobin for his sensitive and scrupulous help in preparing the text for printing.

1

The Political Apprenticeship

Birth and background promised Seán Lemass at least a comfortable if not necessarily a contented life. They gave little hint of the crowded career to come. Middle-class, commercial Catholic Dublin at the end of the nineteenth century knew its place. It had limited horizons, pretentions and ambitions. It appeared a modest enough, cosy, provincial world; for one historian, capital of a country slumbering in a contented 'sort of crease in time'; for a distinguished literary contemporary, 'the city of failure, of rancour, of unhappiness'.[1]

The Lemass family had no such feelings towards Dublin. They had travelled far from their remote French Huguenot origins by the time they finally came to Ireland via Scotland in 1820. They established a successful drapery business in Armagh and then moved to Dublin. John Lemass, hatter, is listed at 2 Capel Street for the first time in the *Dublin Directory* for 1868. He appears to have taken over the hat manufacturing business previously run by Mrs Mary Anne Norman at that address and is not listed among Dublin hatters prior to that date. Trade flourished and John Lemass's Parnellite sympathies earned him a place on Dublin Corporation. In turn, his son, John Timothy Lemass, was born into the business at 2 Capel Street, beside the Essex Bridge. This jovial, dapper hatter inherited his father's business and his Irish parliamentary loyalties. In 1896 he married Frances Phelan of Tulore, Co. Offaly and brought his bride home to live over the shop. Their first child, Noel, was born there but Mrs Lemass, a young woman with a mind of her own, wanted a more salubrious location for her family. Despite the family doctor's view that the city air, redolent of the nearby Liffey at low tide, was good for children, she moved for a period of months to

Ballybrack on the southern side of Dublin Bay. There, in
[2] Norwood Cottage, on 15 July 1899 her second child was
born. He was christened in the nearby Catholic Church of
SS Alphonsus and Columba and given the names John Francis.
He was to make his name as Seán Lemass.

Soon the family moved back to the city but as Mrs Lemass's
carefully spaced children arrived at regular two-yearly intervals,
they changed address more than once. Over time and with
prosperity, they could afford to move into private houses in
Dublin's better residential areas. Like similar Dublin traders,
the family often lived above the shop, familiar alike with the
men below, carefully polishing high-hats for customers, and
the paired succession of live-in maids who helped with house-
hold chores. Pleasures were simple. The younger children
would be walked up most days to the Phoenix Park; sometimes
the more adventurous older boys would help their younger
sisters to 'scut' a free ride on a Guinness dray as it trundled
along the quays. For the summer season, mother, children
and help would fill large trunks and move out to the seaside
at Skerries. There, shared games and activities with families
of a similar class forged friendships that lasted a lifetime.

Education, too, followed an established class pattern.
Neither parochial schools nor the local Christian Brothers
round the corner at Strand Street (who had taught William
Rooney and Arthur Griffith) were acceptable. Instead, the
young Lemass went to the Holy Faith Convent, Haddington
Road, which catered for young ladies and little boys. A
dominant educational influence there was the formidable
Sister Marcella; in later years she would show Seán Lemass
letters from another rising political star, Brendan Bracken.

At the age of nine, after four years in the convent school,
he transferred to the Christian Brothers, O'Connell School,
North Richmond Street. Remembered as a studious boy,
though with a keen interest in football, in 1915 he sat the
Junior Grade, Intermediate and achieved a first-class distinction.
But his school career was soon to end. He moved briefly from
the Christian Brothers to Rosse College but left some time
before the Easter Rising of 1916.

Already the young boy was being drawn from the conventional educational path pursued by other ambitious young

men of his class and generation. He was destined for more active participation in a period of accelerating change in Irish life. Some inkling of this is reflected in his childhood memory of a caucus meeting in 1906 or 1907 held in the back of the Capel Street shop. His father and a group of other Irish party supporters debated whether to oppose a candidate whom they considered unsuitable but who had been nominated by the leaders; 'they all went out of the shop in a group, like aristocrats walking to the guillotine, with their faces set and their fists clenched, pale and drawn-looking, determined to do this thing which was a mortal sin for anyone involved in politics in those days. But they did it; they voted against the party.'[2]

As a boy with the Christian Brothers, Seán Lemass's political inclinations were considerably more radical than his father's parliamentary nationalism. A heady mixture of cultural nationalism and political rhetoric was pushing a new generation beyond home rule. At school, with a cohort of Christian Brothers boys preparing (however unconsciously) to take over from the Clongowes men, he was learning 'the four Rs – reading, 'riting, 'rithmetic and revolution'.[3] At home, an employee in his father's shop, Pat Mullen, was actively involved in the Volunteers and encouraged the boy to join up. According to Lemass's own account:

I told him I didn't think I was old enough to join and he said – 'Well, you look a great deal older than you are and this will be a white lie anyway'.[4]

So at the age of fifteen and a half, he became a member of A Company of the third battalion of the Volunteers.

Shortly afterwards, a new commandant was appointed to the battalion. He made an immediate impression on the young Volunteer when he came to address a parade of A Company in York Street:

My impression of him was of a long, thin fellow with knee breeches and a tweed hat. But he had, of course, enormous personal magnetism and the capacity to hold that crowd of Volunteers there while he addressed them at inordinate length as he always did. There was not a movement among the crowd until he had finished. It impressed me enormously, notwithstanding what I thought was his rather queer-looking appearance.

It was Lemass's first meeting with the man he was to work with for so long, and eventually succeed, Eamon de Valera.

Seán Lemass almost missed the Easter Rising. But the good fortune which marked so many important stages in his political career was there at the beginning. He was not one of the privileged few privy to the plans and it seems possible that his father had arranged with Pat Mullen to keep both his sons from direct involvement. When the 'parade' scheduled for Easter Sunday was cancelled, the Lemass brothers arranged to go hiking next day towards Glencree. They were accompanied by Ken and Jimmy O'Dea (the comedian who would subsequently act as best man at Seán Lemass's wedding). On the way home at Rathfarnham, they met Eóin Mac Néill, titular head of the Volunteers, cycling with his two sons with whom they were acquainted. Ironically, it was from the depressed account of their commander-in-chief that they got their first news of the Rising and information on the posts which were occupied.

The Lemass brothers determined not to be left out; they were not to be deterred by disapproval either from Mac Néill or their parents. There were no trams running from Rathfarnham, so they walked to the nearest Volunteer position identified by Mac Néill at Jacob's biscuit factory. They were not known and not admitted. Early next morning they tried again. They made enquiries at the nearest garrison to home in the Four Courts and were told that the third battalion was somewhere in Ringsend. They never reached de Valera at Boland's Mills. Passing the GPO, a Volunteer friend, Hugh Holohan, on sentry duty told them not to waste their time and brought them into the Post Office. Noel was sent across to the Imperial Hotel. Seán, armed with a shotgun and a basket of home-made bombs, manufactured from billy cans with slow-burning fuses, was posted to the roof of the GPO. In retrospect, he took a less than heroic view of his experiences. He fired a few shots but, since the expected mass attack by British troops never materialised, was not required to hurl any of the bombs from the parapet. During the evacuation, he somehow exchanged the shotgun for a Martini rifle and also acquired a bayonet – probably from a more prudent particip- [5] ant carefully avoiding an ill-conceived bayonet attack on the British.[5] He joined other similarly armed Volunteers in a warehouse yard behind Moore Street.

Looking back on a memorable experience, Lemass recalled the exhaustion as much as the exhilaration of youth:

> During the week I had eaten very little and slept hardly at all. Surprising enough, however, while waiting in the yard, I experienced both hunger and fatigue. I ate a tin of preserved fruit from a shop through which we had passed, and while seated on the stairway into the yard, watching the obstacles being removed, I fell asleep for a few moments.
>
> When I awoke, Seán MacDermott had come into the yard and had begun to address us, to tell us of the decision to surrender. He spoke briefly but very movingly and many of those present were weeping. Some time after he had departed, we were paraded in single column and marched out of the yard into Moore Street, headed by Captain M. W. O'Reilly and a Volunteer bearing a white flag.[6]

After a night in the open in the grounds of the Rotunda Hospital, Lemass was lodged with other Volunteers in the Richmond Barracks in Inchicore. According to a family recollection, Mrs Lemass went to urge her young son's release; Liam Skinner attributes it to the intervention of a 'Dublin Metropolitan Police constable – who knew the Lemass family and had constituted himself the boy's guardian'. According to the *Irish Times Sinn Féin Rebellion Handbook*, 'John Lemas [sic] Dublin' was one of 206 prisoners whose cases were fully investigated and who were then released. Lemass's own account was that after the leaders had been weeded out and the older men deported, a group of fifteen to twenty young fellows of his own age remained. About a fortnight after the Rising they were released.

He was welcomed at home. Any family hope that he might resume his studies was unreal. He had rubbed shoulders with a group of men, the Pearse brothers, Connolly, MacDermott, Ashe, all marked by destiny; however fleeting or slight that contact, it permanently directed the course of his career. For

a few months he returned to Rosse College to study for matric-
ulation in order to satisfy his father's wish that he become a
barrister. But at the earliest opportunity he relinquished the
school desk for the Volunteer movement.

Initially he joined Col. Maurice Moore's private volunteers
on the basis that it gave him military skill and training. With
the re-organisation of the Volunteers proper he moved over,
with his rather inadequate rifle, to the C Company, second
battalion of the Dublin Brigade. His previous experience and
training, combined with native talent, quickly assured promotion over men older than himself. By late 1917 he was
elected lieutenant. Although now working in his father's shop,
his time was increasingly taken up with Volunteer activities.
He spent great effort in training and preparing his men for any
coming struggle, regularly holding all-night exercises in the
North Co. Dublin during the curfew. He was one of two
delegates from his company sent to the Dublin Brigade convention in 1919 with a resolution demanding that they be
allowed to carry arms openly. There was ill-feeling when
the matter was not mentioned. This was investigated by Liam
Lynch; he called Lemass to a conference at 44 North Great
George's Street and told him the resolution had been referred
to general headquarters. Two weeks later the resolution was
approved and it became general practice to carry arms on
parades.

Lemass was always reluctant to talk about his activities
during the War of Independence and Civil War. It was only
with a small band of old cronies that he would reminisce
privately. Publicly he refused to discuss this militant phase.

It is certain that Lemass and his company were engaged in
a number of shooting incidents. He was reportedly involved
in a number of arms raids, directed and commanded the
recovery of £500 worth of jewellery from a gang of armed
robbers, and was active in the Belfast boycott.[7] As the struggle
intensified, so did the Volunteers' tactics; Lemass's own
comment is eloquent:

the time the Black and Tan War became active the numbers
began to shrink very rapidly. The enormous companies
that we commanded during the conscription period began

to dissipate very quickly when it became a different type of operation. Some of them had quite conscientious objections to the type of work we were engaged in and dropped out for that reason.

In the late months of 1920 he acted as captain but on a visit home in December he was captured and interned in Ballykinlar.

Released on the signing of the Treaty, Lemass was immediately involved in the debate that was dividing the country. His own Volunteer company met and was visited and addressed by various officers of the Dublin Brigade. The argument continued, and Lemass only began to make up his own mind after the Treaty was accepted by the Dáil. The break was not immediate. He served for a brief time as training officer to the new Gárda Síochána at their temporary headquarters in the Royal Dublin Society premises in Ballsbridge. When his first pay cheque revealed that this was drawn on the Provisional Government rather than Dáil Éireann, he resigned and joined a group of fellow anti-Treaty training officers at Beggar's Bush barracks. As the division in the army and in the country drifted into civil war, Lemass and the group reported to Rory O'Connor who was gathering anti-Treaty forces in Gardiner Row. Within days the Four Courts was occupied and Lemass moved into that garrison.[8]

It is indicative of Lemass's standing that he was appointed adjutant to the Four Courts commandant, Paddy O'Brien. Bob Briscoe, meeting him for the first time, found 'a very energetic, very pugnacious young cock, short and stocky, with a ruddy skin and black hair'; Todd Andrews recalled:

Lemass was notable for being extremely smartly dressed by any guerilla standards. He was reserved in manner, a characteristic which helped him to maintain strict discipline on army barrack lines.

Ernie O'Malley remembers him as an efficient, busy officer in the Four Courts, patrolling for information and damage inspection. On the one hand, he was ready to blow up the building rather than hand it over; on the other, concerned that younger men had been posted to the munitions area, a dangerous target during the bombardment. When the Four

Courts, inevitably, surrendered he marched out with his men to initial imprisonment in the Jameson Distillery yard.

[8]

If good fortune had first admitted Lemass to the GPO at a dramatic moment in Irish historical development and subsequently arranged his release, it did not desert him now. The Four Courts' location was a powerful symbol for all on the anti-Treaty side. Lemass was there. But he was not for long to endure a consequent loss of freedom.

Marched up to the distillery yard in Stoneybatter, Lemass typically lost no time in scrubbing and tidying himself up. He also carefully checked his surroundings and discovered an escape route through a small gate and the manager's house. He passed the word to a small group and together they walked out to freedom. Frustrated in an effort to join the Wicklow Brigade under Andy MacDonnell in Bray, they joined up with a Tipperary contingent in Blessington and were involved in a number of engagements in south-east Leinster, including the capture of Ferns and Enniscorthy. There was, in Lemass's own phrase, 'a great deal of misdirection and a lack of firm leadership'. Returning to Blessington, Lemass escaped capture and, accompanied by Tom Derrig, walked back to Dublin. In a rapidly deteriorating military situation, the Irregulars again attempted to re-group and re-organise. In the autumn months of 1922 Lemass was appointed Director of Communications and worked to establish an intelligence network. He also picked up the strands of his private life and arranged from time to time to see the girl he was to marry, Kathleen Hughes. Circumstances were increasingly difficult. A planned attack on the CID centre at Oriel House did not materialise and in December 1922 Lemass was arrested near O'Connell Street and interned at Harepark Camp, the Curragh and Mountjoy.

His experiences in the Civil War and during his imprisonment noticeably toughened the shell of the young man. He became a 'typical IRA hard man', impatient of politicians, not unduly sensitive to the feelings of his companions, unwilling to complain about the harshness of his treatment and unshaken in his confidence. It was also in this period that he developed his broader interest in public affairs and began to read any books he could lay hands on dealing with economics. Internment, so often the university of the revolutionary, was transforming the young rebel into a student. His political apprenticeship had begun. But, for the moment, he [9] was a prisoner of war eager for freedom.

An attempted escape tunnel was discovered and led to harsh treatment in the Curragh's Glasshouse, handcuffed to a wall-rack with toes barely touching the ground. But their lives were probably spared as a result of de Valera's cease-fire order. Lemass and other leaders were moved to Mountjoy and at first lodged in a basement 'which was not exactly a rest home'. Fate again intervened to secure an early release – this time in a cruelly intimate shape. Lemass's popular older brother, Noel, had disappeared some time earlier. His dead body, badly abused, was now discovered in the Dublin mountains; the CID was generally believed responsible. Seán was released in October 1923 to attend the funeral and immediately resumed his active career. From here onwards, however, its direction was increasingly political.

Lemass, like many young men of his generation, had been attracted by the promise of early action. Intolerant of the patient incrementalism of the home rule movement, conscious of the criticism of party politics, they had turned their back on constitutional agitation in favour of propaganda of the deed. In the aftermath of military defeat, they began the process of political re-education.

The transition, though relatively rapid, cannot have been easy. Lemass was still an IRA man, and retained some of the typical Volunteer's disdain for and suspicion of the political wing of the republican movement. He had never been a member of the old Sinn Féin political organisation.[9] His election to the Standing Committee of Sinn Féin was virtually an emotional reaction by the ard fheis of 1923; the meeting had been suspended to allow delegates to attend the funeral of Noel Lemass. On their return, without consulting the newly-released Seán Lemass, they elected him to the party's senior hierarchy; he only discovered what had happened through a newspaper.[10] It is perhaps indicative of his own sense of priorities at the time that he readily reconciled himself to this political appointment on the grounds that it was appropriate to his main function as Director of Intelligence in the Dublin Brigade. But the IRA was already in decline and

over the next few months the young man was drawn inexor-
[10] ably away from the military and into the political area of
republican activity.

First, as though signalling his civilian rehabilitation, he
returned to his father's business and married Kathleen Hughes.
It was not a match that pleased the bride's family. The families
were friendly through summer holidays spent in Skerries.
Kathleen had begun by writing to Seán while he was a prisoner
and they had managed to snatch a few brief meetings while
he was on the run. But, reasonably enough, the Hughes family
were not enthusiastic about entrusting their daughter's future
to a recently released prisoner with no very clear prospects
who continued to be involved in the less than respectable
world of IRA-Sinn Féin activity. They could not be expected
to recognise the public destiny and private contentment
marked out in these unpromising beginnings.

Lemass quickly became an active and assiduous member of
the standing committee of Sinn Féin, served as a trouble
shooter and cut his teeth as a political organiser. He does not
appear to have been afraid of controversy; he seconded a
motion — essentially a criticism of a fellow member — 'that
Sinn Féin, being a non-sectarian body, the question of religious
opinions of a member should be no bar to their candidature.'[11]
There was a hint of his future practical sense of administration
in his own motion proposing 'a more systematic organisation'
to deal with 'the economic distress of released prisoners'. His
colleagues' awareness of Lemass's organisational capacity is
reflected in his early appointment to a variety of committees:
to arrange a reception for a released prisoner; to organise
trains for the Liam Lynch anniversary; to make arrangements
for the Dublin Brigade's commemoration parade and the
Dublin Comhairle Ceanntair Easter Sunday celebrations.
Lemass's own interests are reflected in efforts to secure
Labour votes and to develop economic policies on industrial
relations and rural labour conditions.

Lemass had clearly established a name and position for
himself in the anti-Treaty third Sinn Féin and must have been
regarded as a likely candidate for electoral success. It is difficult
to reconcile the record of his active involvement in party
affairs with his own account that he was not even consulted

before being selected for the vacancy in the South Dublin constituency created by the death of Deputy Philip Cosgrave.[12] [11] It may be that his consent was taken for granted. At all events, in retrospect, he considered this first campaign very inefficient; in particular he regarded his comrades' efforts to organise personation teams on his behalf as less useful than the more conventional door-to-door canvas. Nevertheless, in a small turnout on Wednesday 12 March 1924, his challenge to a well-known opponent was impressive enough.[13]

A second election in the same constituency was not long delayed. Hugh Kennedy, the attorney-general, resigned his seat on his appointment as Chief Justice. Cumann na nGaedheal nominated Seamus Hughes; Sinn Féin again chose Lemass. This time he determined to take charge of the campaign himself. The somewhat sparse newspaper accounts give some indication of a campaign strategy that was both energetic in organisation and radical in tone. At a meeting in College Green a crowd of 'several thousands' heard him proclaim:

> that when the Republicans came into control of the machinery of government they would see that it moved in the interests of the whole Irish people and not in the interests of a small privileged class. They cared nothing for the old catch-cries about the rights of property and the sacredness of interests.[14]

At an eve of the poll rally in College Street, with three platforms, Lemass was equally emphatic in enunciating republican principles; although perhaps significantly as a basis for stability:

> Mr Lemass said that compromise had failed and that their object was complete independence for the whole country. That was the only way to secure stability. The Council for the Unemployed held a meeting on the same evening, in support of his candidacy, at Foster Place.

The result, on 18 November 1924, helped to found Lemass's subsequent reputation as a political organiser. While his opponent, in a two-sided contest, gained five hundred votes, Lemass secured an extra two and a half thousand and won the seat. The *Irish Times* leader-writer commented on the apathy of

government supporters and the success of the Republicans
in getting out the vote.[15]

Election entitled Lemass to a place in Comhairle na
dTeachtaí, the Council of Deputies regarded by Republicans
as the actual legitimate government of Ireland. It was a
nebulous body, a shadow of the old unified cabinet of the
original Dáil, whose mantle of authority it claimed.[16] It was
indicative of Lemass's reputation in both the political and
military wings of the movement that he was chosen to succeed
Aiken as titular Minister for Defence. Although he subsequently
claimed credit for maintaining the convention of civil control
of the armed forces, the reality was disillusioning. The body
had no power, the Minister for Defence had no effective
authority and what little money was available soon evapor-
ated. The shadow government soon lost the reluctant alleg-
iance of the IRA. At a general army convention in Bullock
Castle, Dalkey on 14 November 1925, all connections with
the Dáil were severed. Lemass had little regard for this
rump IRA's dream of another offensive campaign. He was
increasingly conscious of the need to organise and mobilise
public opinion. The break with the army mirrored growing
tensions in his attitude to, and relations with, Sinn Féin.

When de Valera attempted to rationalise the Sinn Féin
executive by proposing five sub-committees, he had appointed
Lemass both to the organisation and the economics groupings.[17] At this stage it is evident Lemass was interested in
moving the Sinn Féin party beyond simply its constitutional
disagreement with Cumann na nGaedheal and persuading it
to adopt distinct and advanced social and economic policies. It
seems that this was not acceptable. In February 1925 his
report on the work of the economics sub-committee included
a proposal to circulate the economics programme of the
Australian Labour Party; a month later 'Seán Lemass tendered
his resignation from the economic committee as other work
prevented his attendance'[18]

This 'other work' took two forms: a concentration on party
re-organisation in the Dublin area[19] and increasing efforts to
move Sinn Féin to a more flexible and pragmatic political
strategy. An indication of this direction was the resolution
passed at a special meeting of the standing committee, at

which ard chomhairle delegates were present:

[13]

> that the President may act on the assumption that the
> question of Republicans entering the Free State 'parliam-
> ent' if the oath were removed, is an open question, to be
> decided on its merits when the question arises as a practical
> issue.

Although according to the garbled reports of Free State
intelligence sources, Lemass was still numbered among the
extreme element of the political group, he had moved far
from his early militancy.[20]

He was one of a small group willing to recognise the continuing decline in the party's fortunes, whether measured in
terms of finances, membership or the capacity to attract
votes.[21] In a remarkable series of six articles in Sinn Féin's
weekly paper, *An Phoblacht*, Lemass offered an analysis
of the party's weakness. [22] The series also revealed at this very
early stage of his political career some of his most enduring
characteristics: a frankness bordering on brutality; a pragmatism unhampered by sentiment; a willingness to cut procedural
corners and to take calculated risks; an attachment to decision
and action; and a total absence of the fear of failure.

Lemass drew on his experience as chairman of the Dublin
Reorganisation Committee in his critique. He urged younger
members to 'weed out the "duds" — alike those who have
outlived their utility and those who were always useless' and
take over the leadership. He defined what Sinn Féin meant for
him in terms he could still echo forty years later:

> the policy of self-reliance. . . . it means doing ourselves
> what should be done and not merely criticising others for
> their neglect. . . . building the foundations of a National and
> Prosperous Ireland — FROM THE BOTTOM. It means helping
> in every enterprise that promises good for our country, no
> matter by whom that enterprise is initiated, or who will
> profit by it.

The precarious and artificial unity of the third Sinn Féin
survived the ard fheis of November 1925 but increasingly the
gap between the zealous republican idealist and realistic
political pragmatists widened. For one group, the oath was an

insurmountable ideological obstacle; for the other, the search for an 'intermediate objective' intensified. In December 1925, the signing of the Boundary Agreement inspired a further attempted political initiative. On 8 December, de Valera and 38 Republican TDs met with Labour deputies and others to discuss how the measure might be opposed but this 'Shelbourne Parliament' failed to reach agreement. After the Boundary crisis, the futility of abstention became more widely recognised. The need for decision – even at the expense of party unity – became more urgent. De Valera still exercised his customary caution. At a meeting in Ranelagh on 6 January 1926, he announced publicly that he was prepared to enter the Free State Dáil if there was no oath to be taken. A week later, the party decided to call a special ard fheis in March to determine the issues.

Lemass continued his articles in *An Phoblacht*. By now he was virtually inviting schism in the party. Some of this rhetoric seemed designed to drive de Valera from debate to decision:

> there are some who would have us sit at the roadside and debate abstruse points about a de jure this and a de facto that, but the reality we want is away in the distance – and we cannot get there unless we move.

This provoked a sharp reply from Brian Fagan, the secretary of Sinn Féin. Undeterred, Lemass argued the case for an immediate and practical objective. In his sixth article, 'The Will to Win', he asserted that

> the first essential requisite of freedom is the determination to achieve it. Those who place their trust in blind choice, or in the benevolence of Providence, may sometimes succeed but those who are in earnest always do.

By now the strains within Sinn Féin were telling. In a letter to *An Phoblacht* on 19 February 1926, Fagan warned readers against the half-truths in Lemass's arguments. The idea of a new phase as decisive was, he said, 'false national philosophy'. The examples of Tone, Davis and Pearse illustrated the fallacy in Lemass's assertion that those in earnest always succeed. Fagan rejected the 'hard-headed practical men' and argued:

there is no real antagonism between ideals and practice, but there is an apparent antagonism created by men who [15] deny ideals or betray them in the name of expediency. Without ideals there can be no true practice.

The editor, P. J. Ruttledge, appended a note that this correspondence was now closed 'as some people considered it was touching too close upon the issues to be decided at the ard fheis'. But Lemass squeezed in a final reply before the special ard fheis, in the issue of 26 February 1926, which practically demanded either takeover or the creation of a new political party. He agreed with Fagan that no one should 'quit' but claimed 'that any group, or section, or party, that finds it has outlived its utility, and that it has become a hindrance and not a help in the fight has a duty to stand out of the way — to quit.' He took the view that if Sinn Féin idealists could not adapt to new conditions, they should stand aside: 'of what use are ideals if they do not spur us to action? Action alone will justify our faith.'[23]

That action was now imminent. The split in the third Sinn Féin would create a new political party, Fianna Fáil. Lemass played a central part in the creation and strengthening of the political machine that was to sweep him into three decades of office as minister and finally as Taoiseach.

2
The Parliamentary Journeyman

Seán Lemass was still technically employed in his father's shop. He needed the weekly 'wage' of £4 to keep his small family going in a rented flat in Terenure. But the decade from 1916 to 1926 had been an inescapable introduction to the trade of politics. He had experienced the reality of military activity and defeat, recognising the mood of public disapproval, and rejected the IRA's threat of renewed war. Politically, he had advanced rapidly through his position in Sinn Féin and his status as a member of Comhairle na dTeachtaí and minister; his involvement sharpened his critique.

> Sinn Féin by this time had become a collection of not merely dedicated people but of various cranks of one kind or another. The public image of Sinn Féin was being affected by this galaxy of cranks around it — so that the foundation of a new movement which could cut clear of this accumulation of queer people was not unattractive.

To achieve it required more attainable policies, better organisation and an effective leader. Lemass was to be involved in all three areas.

Gradually the policy emphasis had shifted to the idea of the abolition of the oath as an intermediate objective. But de Valera, with his customary caution, was reluctant to commit himself publicly to a political initiative which was certain to be divisive within the party. Lemass, perhaps more than anyone else, was instrumental in forcing the issue but he was not alone. He could not have retained his position in Sinn Féin without considerable support; he needed the co-operation of P. J. Ruttledge to publicise his concerns, and was recognised as a protege of de Valera. The relationship between the two men lasted a lifetime. If the older de Valera appreciated the talent, energy and enthusiasm of Lemass, the younger [17] responded with a loyalty and respect he accorded few others. If in the critical months preceding the foundation of Fianna Fáil, Lemass was the public spur, it is evident that de Valera was not unwilling to be prodded. Indeed, as Lemass himself later acknowledged, while he worked hard to gain support for de Valera's formula on the oath at Sinn Féin's special ard fheis, he was never sure whether de Valera wanted an adverse vote or not; he reported that de Valera was not upset by his narrow defeat.[1]

At the special ard fheis of March 1926, de Valera moved to resolve:

> That once the admission oath of the twenty-six-county and six-county assemblies is removed, it becomes a question not of principle but of policy whether or not Republican representatives should attend these assemblies.

This clearly split the 'principled' Republican fundamentalists from the 'realist' politicians. Some delegates appear to have become converted to the new departure but had been advised by de Valera supporters to obey their cumainn instructions and vote on principle.[2] This may give substance to Lemass's doubts whether de Valera seriously intended to carry his proposal.

Once the break occurred Lemass had no doubts what to do. It was time to break with the past, with the 'cranks' who now dominated Sinn Féin; time to found a new party. In later years, de Valera underlined that it was Lemass who recommended this course; he recalled:

> On that day in March 1926, I happened to be walking out of the Rathmines Town Hall with Seán Lemass. I had just resigned as president of Sinn Féin and I said to him, 'Well, Seán, I have done my best, but I have been beaten. Now that is the end for me. I am leaving public life.' Seán was shocked to hear me saying this, and he said: 'But you are not going to leave us now Dev, at this stage. You cannot leave us like that. We have to go on now. We must form a new organisation along the policy lines you suggested at the ard fheis. It is the only way forward.' We discussed it

further and at last I told him that I could not but agree with his logic and said I would do all the necessary things. But we were only a few people and we hadn't a penny between us.[3]

De Valera's official biographer has recorded that Lemass took the initiative which led to the formation of a new political party.[4] It was he who gathered the pro-de Valera members of the Sinn Féin standing committee for a formal break with the party and who then convened the meeting, at the old Sinn Féin headquarters in 23 Suffolk Street on Good Friday 1926, which formed the new party. But Lemass failed to dissuade de Valera from adopting the title Fianna Fáil: he argued for an unambiguous proclamation, 'The Republican Party', and said people would not understand the Gaelic title and that opponents would distort the Irish letters 'Fáil' into the English word 'Fail'; finally they agreed a compromise — Fianna Fáil (the Republican Party).

As the work of organising the new party got under way, Lemass was surprised to discover that the apparently evenly divided ard fheis was not representative of Sinn Féin sentiment at local level. He told Michael Mills:

It was assumed, of course, that the ard fheis, which rejected de Valera's policy, represented the majority of Sinn Féin opinion throughout the country. But when we started to organise Fianna Fáil we found this was not so. Within a year of the first Fianna Fáil executive being set up, we had a nationwide organisation, the strongest in the country, fully geared for action with cumainn and county executives everywhere. The speed with which the Fianna Fáil organisation came into being, from a group sitting in Dublin to a nationwide organisation extending to every parish in the country was quite phenomenal.

It was not done without effort. De Valera himself was active together with other leaders, but it was Lemass, as a member of the original organising committee and subsequently as joint honorary secretary (with Gerry Boland), who carried the greatest burden. He was, in T. P. O'Neill's phrase, 'the driving genius'. He was the principal organiser, travelling up and down the country, often drawing on his old IRA and Sinn Féin communications' networks to identify local leaders who could attract support to the new party. It was a period of intensive work. The family remember nights and weekends away from home. It was a routine that became a way of life over the next half-dozen years. Until Fianna Fáil entered the Dáil in 1927, he was still dependent on what he could earn in his father's shop; once he took his seat, he became a full-time politician — his deputy's allowance supplemented by a small payment from party funds. Fortunately, his wife had the managerial capacity to keep the growing family on this income.[5]

Although not yet properly documented, Lemass's work in organising the new Fianna Fáil is acknowledged. It was a task he relished; the objectives were clear, the results measurable. He retained little memory of the detail, beyond a much repeated story of recruiting Neil Blaney (father of the later minister) and the marvel of the family at a stranger coming to the front door when the farmer himself was working on a hay-rick. Generally, he remembered careering round Ireland in a tin lizzy, concentrating on the recruitment of 'sound' republicans around whom local organisations could be developed. Political opinions had already been formed, disagreement on the basic Treaty issue had deepened into passion, the effort of organisation was not so much to convert people to the republican cause as expounded by Fianna Fáil but to get them actively involved in supporting the party. With every gain, the apathy he had already identified with the hopelessly idealistic ideology of Sinn Féin was replaced by a practical expectation of success.

The reality of Fianna Fáil's strength was reflected in the electoral history of those years. As an American observer noted, 'every politician in Ireland had put his house in order in anticipation of the general election of 1927'.[6] The government party, Cumann na nGaedheal, used a special committee to examine its own electoral machinery; Labour revised its organisation to extend its appeal to non-trade-unionists; two new parties, the National League and Clann Éireann, were ready to compete with other small groupings and independents of many shades. Fianna Fáil would have no easy passage in this first contest and the absence of de Valera in the United States through the early months of the year was not helpful.

Rumours of possible alliances between Fianna Fáil, Clann Éireann and the IRA surfaced in the press; Lemass had a private meeting on the latter issue with Peadar O'Donnell but finally all sides went their own way.[7] It was an exhausting and exhaustive campaign. Fianna Fáil nominated eighty-seven candidates for the 153 Dáil seats and Lemass, as main organiser, spent most of his time in Dublin and the eastern part of the country. The outcome more than justified the break with Sinn Féin. The new Fianna Fáil won 26 per cent of the first-preference vote and 44 seats. It also meant that with one per cent less than the Sinn Féin vote in 1923, Fianna Fáil secured the same number of seats. And Seán Lemass headed the poll in his constituency, over 300 votes ahead of his nearest rival.

Overall, the results of this June 1927 election were inconclusive. But, in rapid succession, the assassination of Kevin O'Higgins and the Electoral Amendment Bill, requiring candidates on nomination to agree to take the oath, soon resolved the central issue. De Valera led his party through a charade of subscribing to the oath, as required by Article 17 of the Constitution, and Fianna Fáil took their seats in the Dáil. Immediately the Labour Party put down a motion of no confidence. When a National League deputy, Alderman John Jinks of Sligo, failed to show up for the division, the result was a tie. The casting vote of the Ceann Comhairle saved the government but a new election was inevitable and after a few days, the government announced the dissolution of the Dáil.

The campaign for the September election was short and sharp. All parties entered the fray with depleted funds and this undoubtedly affected the smaller groupings disproportionately. Even Labour had to cut back its candidates from fifty to twenty-eight. The two main parties made considerable use of newspaper advertising in addition to the more traditional campaigning methods of meetings and canvassing. Lemass, still maintaining connections with the IRA organisation and consciously seeking support from Labour voters, was ready to sweep up the remnants of Clann Éireann support but his effort to include Dr Pat McCartan on the Fianna Fáil panel in his constituency was apparently vetoed by de Valera.[8] The results of the election strengthened both Cumann na nGaedheal and Fianna Fáil at the expense of the smaller parties and more clearly than ever defined the cleavage that would continue to determine the shape of Irish politics through the twentieth century. Cumann na nGaedheal almost matched its performance of 1923 with 38.4 per cent of the first-preference vote and 62 seats. But Fianna Fáil remained close with 34.9 per cent of the vote and 57 seats. Lemass increased his own vote by over 2,700 and again headed the poll, this time 1,800 votes ahead of his nearest rival.

With party margins so close there was a great inducement for a man like Lemass to push his party to the front, and for the next five years the work of organisation occupied much of his time and energy. He told Liam O'Doherty that 'he had not seen Dublin on a Sunday for three years' and subsequently looked back on the period as the most exhausting phase of his career.[9] This was scarcely surprising for he combined this party activity with his new role as parliamentarian.

While some attention has been paid to Lemass's contribution to the growing organisational and electoral strength of Fianna Fáil, his early parliamentary career has been largely ignored. The tendency has been to concentrate on the party man and the minister; to forget the sheer scale of his parliamentary involvement. Yet, even adopting a crude measure, a cursory examination of the Dáil debates shows Lemass speaking more often and on a wider range of issues than other Irish parliamentarians of his generation. Only two features of his initial years in the Dáil have attracted any notice: first, his description of Fianna Fáil as 'a slightly constitutional party'; second, his reputation as a man who refused to use the bitter, acrimonious, and often highly personal invective of Civil War rhetoric in parliamentary deabte. Taken together, they give an incomplete and highly misleading impression of an important phase in Lemass's political development; each requires closer scrutiny.

Lemass's description of Fianna Fáil as 'a slightly constitutional party' needs to be placed in context. As soon as they took their seats in the Dáil, Fianna Fáil launched a campaign to secure the release of republican prisoners held since the Civil War. They also repeatedly charged that the gardaí, and more particularly the Special Branch, were engaged in a campaign of harrassment and intimidation against republican sympathisers and Fianna Fáil supporters. Lemass played an active part in this sustained opposition campaign. But he was also careful to express his views, in the words of one opponent, 'quietly, dispassionately, and without heat or the conscious giving of offence to anyone'.[10]

Lemass opened his very first speech in the Dáil with an attack on Cumann na nGaedheal's continuing use of the Public Safety Act.[11] He argued that governmental coercion contributed to instability; that it was used for party advantage; that it threatened to rekindle 'the dying embers of the fires of civil strife'. He redefined the issue of the Treaty:

> What does it matter whether we stand to maintain the Treaty or not? We do stand for reorganising the Irish people and strengthening their will to resume their advance to the complete independence of a united Ireland. If we get from the people the necessary power, and if it can be done with safety to the nation, we do intend to alter the Treaty and to alter the Constitution, wherever they are in conflict with the national interests.

And he argued that national unity was a prerequisite for economic reconstruction and urged all deputies to co-operate 'in wiping out the recollection of the hatred, the bitterness and the jealousies that were created in this country after the Civil War'.

But, if he seemed prepared to commit himself and the party to the democratic process, a certain ambiguity remained in attitudes towards the legitimacy of the state and the Constitution. Lemass may have become a pragmatic politician; he remained a 'republican' by inclination. On the annual Army Bill in 1927, he argued against a 'hard shell' standing army 'easily cracked by superior force', declaring a preference for a 'soft one' on which military blows would have little effect and which would 'make it impossible for any outside authority to rule with comfort in this island'.[12] He also identified the likely *casus belli:* 'aggression on the part of one power from which our history has taught us to expect it'. Indeed, throughout these early months — and later — Lemass repeatedly raised questions about police harassment, ill-treatment of prisoners and the use of the secret service, which seemed to indicate [23] some reluctance to accept the legitimacy of the Irish Free State. On the estimate for the Department of Justice in 1928,[13] he spoke about discrimination in the administration of justice. He accused the police of raiding active members of Fianna Fáil, planting evidence and provoking breaches of the peace. On the latter point, Lemass added:

> there are emblems and slogans which, when displayed in the streets, have resulted in riots, and, please God, always will. I refer to the flag of the British Empire. There is always work for the police, rioting and broken heads when that emblem is displayed.

On the following day he urged the Dáil to frame regulations for political prisoners on the grounds that they were not in the same class as criminals. Lemass and others constantly raised such issues, thus provoking questions about their own ambiguous attitude towards the institutions of the state.

A five-day debate in private members' time was designed to focus attention on the government's attitudes.[14] Fianna Fáil proposed a select committee 'to review the cases of all prisoners who claim that their cases arise out of the Civil War or, apart from strictly legal considerations, have a political aspect'. But other deputies, while critical of the Cumann na nGaedheal insistence on hardline law-and-order attitudes, expressed doubts about Fianna Fáil's motives. Labour, in particular, may have been stung by Lemass's earlier taunts that 'long association with this House has sapped the vitality of the Labour Party' and created its 'invertebrate attitude'.[15] In the course of his speech, Labour deputy William Davin wondered whether Fianna Fáil was able to distinguish what was legitimate political activity and what was not. He concluded in a similar vein, supporting the proposal in the hope of learning 'the real meaning of constitutional activity as interpreted by the [sic] Fianna Fáil'.

This provoked a retort from Lemass and an exchange:

> I think it would be right to inform Deputy Davin that Fianna Fáil is a slightly constitutional party. We are perhaps

open to the definition of a constitutional party, but, before anything, we are a republican party. We have adopted the method of political agitation to achieve our end, because we believe, in the present circumstances, that method is best in the interests of the nation and of the republican movement, and for no other reason.

Mr T. J. O'Connell: It took you five years to make up your mind.

Mr Lemass: Five years ago, the methods we adopted were not the methods we have adopted now. Five years ago, we were on the defensive; perhaps in time we may recoup our strength sufficiently to go on the offensive. Our objective is to establish a republican government in Ireland. If that can be done by the present methods we have, we will be very pleased, but, if not, we would not confine ourselves to them.

Lemass's remarks certainly suggest a less than wholehearted commitment to democratic processes and reflect a pragmatic willingness to 'go on the offensive' and use force to achieve political aims. The Minister for Industry and Commerce, Patrick McGilligan, chose to see them as an effort by Lemass to restore his standing wth the IRA.[16] But it seems that Lemass, still by his own admission an impatient and inexperienced parliamentarian, was provoked into saying more than he meant; that he blurted out some of the residual frustration of a defeated armed militancy which, at a considered level, he had already abandoned. Certainly, his own gloss on the remark in the Dáil a month later presents Lemass as an essentially constitutional parliamentary politician. Speaking on Fianna Fáil's motion to remove the oath, Lemass deliberately drew down his 'slightly constitutional' comment in order to argue that the Cumann na nGaedheal government — though for different reasons — shared Fianna Fáil's view of the Irish Free State Constitution as 'an intolerable nuisance'; that the people had never been given a chance to give a considered view on the Constitution; that the government's own attitude revealed in amendments, proposed and opposed, 'have shown themselves to be only slightly constitutional as well'.[17]

The Cumann na nGaedheal government's rather cavalier

attitude towards amending the unduly flexible Irish Free State Constitution gave some substance to Lemass's argument. He developed it at some length in debate on amendment no. 17 which he described as a 'bill to abrogate the Constitution.'[18] Lemass argued that extra emergency powers were not required, that they were an incitement to the IRA and a partisan effort to trap Fianna Fáil. Both branches of the old Sinn Féin had maintained curious alliances – Cumann na nGaedheal with the IRB, Fianna Fáil with the IRA – and he asked Independent deputies to judge whether there

> was there any particular virtue in 1923 or 1925 that made them right or made us right in deciding to cease our connection with these organisations?. . . I am not saying that everything in the garden is lovely, that the country is peaceful and the flowers are beautiful, and that there is no need to worry. There is a situation which concerns all of us. . . . We think that the Dáil, before arming itself with jackboots to deal with these people, many of whom, however mistaken they are, hold their convictions quite sincerely, should examine that method.

While some might see in this an unresolved ambiguity towards the use of force to achieve political ends, others would interpret it as a pragmatic effort both to bridge the gap between the major parties and to draw the paramilitaries back into political activity.

On other occasions Lemass went further in upholding the tenuous connection between constitutional authority and extra-parliamentary activity. Despite his contemptuous dismissal of internal Sinn Féin legalistic arguments, he insisted that Comhairle na dTeachtaí had remained true to constitutional principles. When opponents commented on his spell as Minister for Defence, he responded that he exercised political control over the armed forces.[19] If this claim exaggerated the degree of political authority exercised over the IRA, it nevertheless underlined Lemass's desire to maintain the convention of civil control of the army.

There may have been a degree of sophistry in these arguments. McGilligan expressed the government view that there were two Lemasses in the Dáil, the responsible economist and the irreconcilable militant.[20]

[26]   Lemass certainly continued to raise questions about police, security and general political matters that could feed the latter interpretation.[21] But the detailed record of his first parliamentary years sustain the view of an opposition deputy rapidly establishing a formidable reputation for his contributions to debates on economics and public finance. Indeed, his range was even wider, giving rise to pointed remarks from the government side that he was 'acting semi-leader of the opposition'.[22]

The speeches also show something of the development of Lemass's economic philosophy as well as his consistently positive emphasis and pragmatic inclination. He first turned to economic issues in a speech on a Labour motion of relief of unemployment a fortnight after the 1927 Dáil resumed.[23] He demanded emergency measures since the unemployment problem was due to 'the financial system in operation in this country' and urged positive steps to build up domestic investment both by taxing exportable capital and the granting of concessions on income tax on Irish money invested in Ireland and in Irish industries. Above all, he identified what was to become the main thrust of his own policy, protection, which he described as 'one of the keys to the whole situation, because, if we protect our industries, we make it profitable to invest Irish capital in them, and those who control capital are always anxious to find profitable investments.'

He linked advocacy of protection with criticism of the existing Tariff Commission when speaking on his own motion in February 1928. Boldly he asserted that the motion assumed that the question of policy had already been decided; what was now required was adequate machinery. But in the peroration of his opening speech there were hints of economic policy that went well beyond erecting tariff barriers:

> It is essential that we should decide on some definite policy for industrial and agricultural reconstruction and put it into operation in the very near future. . . . We consider that the entire economic policy of the country should be decided on by a national economic council such as exists in Germany and France and such as is suggested by one of

the big English parties for that nation. . . . Until we get a
definite national policy decided on in favour of industrial [27]
and agricultural protection and an executive in office
prepared to enforce that policy, it is useless to hope for
results.[24]

Lemass was already envisaging a far more interventionist
role by the state. He saw protection as part of a co-ordinated
set of policies designed not in the interests of the mercantile
class but in the interests of the community as a whole. At the
same time, he recognised that some manufacturers feared that
protection might make them targets for takeover by foreign
companies and had argued earlier in the speech that Irish
industries must remain 'if not under the control of Irish
capital, at least controlled by capital that would be under
Irish control'.

This closing speech on the motion is an example of
Lemass's effort (more consistent over a long career than has
often been recognised) to marry economic and social policy
management as a direct responsibility of government.[25] He
insisted that even if manufacturers were 'slack or inefficient'
in applying for tariffs, the government should be prepared to
intervene on behalf of workers whose 'interests are of much
greater importance to the nation than the interests of a small
group of owners'. Above all he urged in opposition what he
practised in office: decision and action. 'We must make up our
mind, one way or the other, and having made it up, we must
stick to our decision.'

Advocacy of protection, criticism of the Tariff Commission and attacks on the apathy of the administration
became recurrent themes as Lemass increasingly emerged as
the principal Fianna Fáil spokesman on economic issues.
The speeches revealed both the seminal influence of Arthur
Griffith's Sinn Féin policies on Lemass's nationalism and the
fruits of his enforced study during periods of internment. An
informed and intimate observer of the mature Lemass in
office has recorded the view that 'Griffith's views had a
profound influence on Lemass: they can indeed be said to
have laid the basis of his life's work.'[26] Lemass was also
influenced by another persistent characteristic – an openness

to and interest in developments in the world about him. He attacked the government's reluctance to recognise that everywhere free trade was giving way to protection.[27]

Lemass deployed an arsenal of economic and political arguments. He argued the case for protecting the flour milling industry in terms of encouraging self-reliance, of security of supply in the time of war, and of freedom from both dumping and the operation of international cartels which could defeat governments. Similarly, he argued that 'political freedom was necessary to break out of the British economic system' and should be used to develop the production of cement in Ireland.[28] Lemass stressed that as 'England's biggest customer', Ireland had a strong bargaining counter in trade negotiation.

His attachment to the encouragement of private enterprise in Ireland by protection was balanced by some recognition of its dangers and inadequacies. He was opposed to outright monopoly and argued that 'the operation of the ordinary economic laws' of competition encouraged efficiency.[29] At the same time he recognised the need for vigorous state intervention and criticised the Department of Industry and Commerce for failing to encourage decentralisation, to become involved in running the railways, and to develop a nationalised system of car insurance. He also sought to link economic growth with social policy and seemed to be hinting at more radical solutions.

This note was especially evident in attacks on those in entrenched positions. He spoke about ministerial admissions that the inherited administrative machinery was not ideal and sheltered vested interests.[30] He argued that the Poor Relief (Dublin) Bill 1929 should be interpreted as a vote of censure on the Department of Industry and Commerce for failing to stimulate industrial development and employment. More directly, Lemass suggested:

> a country in which over-production is a disaster and in which unemployment and poverty can exist side by side, has some serious defects in its economic organisation which must be eradicated if any social progress is to be made.

He attacked the preservation of the commercial franchise in Dublin Corporation on the grounds that businessmen were only concerned with profits and giving them special privileges was undemocratic. Lemass also condemned the government in the 1930 Budget debate for supporting millionaires, landlords and the local nabobs, adding: 'We do not want these people here. I think the country would be much better off without them.' Subsequently, when challenged on the grounds that landlords often gave considerable local employment, he managed to modify this while preserving a populist tone; he had no objection to millionaires,

> but I do object to attractions being held out to them for which the poor working men of Dublin have to pay ... I say the first concerns of this Dáil should be to protect the interests and preserve the happiness of the men who build up the wealth of the country, and they are not dukes, earls or millionaires. They are plain, good, honest-to-God, working men whose interests were neglected when this Budget was framed.

Much of what he said reflected a growing consensus on economic policy within Fianna Fáil. As early as 1928, the party published a revised edition of a Dáil speech by de Valera under the title *Fianna Fáil and its Economic Policy*, which encapsulated the main themes of economic self-sufficiency and growth.[31] Lemass regarded himself as the most important influence in the development of the party's economic thinking.[32] But there were divergences in the senior ranks of Fianna Fáil and on occasions Lemass defined his own position with some care. On the 1930 Finance Bill[33] he offered a gloss on MacEntee's charge of 'reckless borrowing' by the government; it was reckless, said Lemass, because it was haphazard, 'and not based upon any considered plan'. On the other hand, he argued with Keynes in favour of 'the wisdom of embarking upon large development schemes during a time of depression and unemployment'. He also repeated the case for government intervention, to break the strong tradition of investing abroad among 'the Irish capitalist class', and to force 'the financial institutions to give a proper lead in the matter when national interests so required'.

This suggestion of compulsion went far beyond any consensus within Fianna Fáil. It may have reflected some of

Lemass's concern that the more radical policies of left-wing groups like Saor Éire were attracting support among younger members.[34] But it was also a useful clue to one of Lemass's deepest political convictions: that it was not enough to enjoy executive power, it must be used. Those were not isolated remarks. Lemass was willing to accept that the adoption of a full protectionist policy would result in some dislocation of trade, that it would not produce an immediate solution to the unemployment problem, no matter how drastically used, but he insisted that increased production targets could be met.

> If we set about that programme with the same vigour and enthusiasm as the Russian government is now applying to the five-years' programme in operation in that country, we would undoubtedly be able to increase our productive capacity, so as to be able to provide the whole of the requirements of the home market in these particular goods at the end of the ten year period. In that way, a permanent solution of the problem of unemployment, as we know it, can be found.

But this somewhat provocatively phrased argument was balanced by a more moderate Keynesian view of the role of government in a mixed economy: that it should intervene only 'when trade is depressed and unemployment is serious'.

That was a model of state intervention closer to Roosevelt than to Stalin. It reflected a pragmatism that was willing to match economic theory with popular appeal. It was part of his public persona as spokesman for the dispossessed, the tribune of the working man, the deputy for Dublin. In his maiden speech on the nomination of Cosgrave as President of the Executive Council, he began by stressing unemployment as a greater problem than subversion.[35] He regularly attacked the Senate as a 'bulwark of imperialism . . . always hostile to the interests of the Irish nation', 'a collection of lords, dukes, earls and people of that kind', which should be made 'as impotent and innocuous as possible'. Repeatedly he pinpointed the conservatism of government policy and the inertia of its administration. He talked about the dilatory policy and incompetence of the government 'and what I call the laziness of the Department of Industry and Commerce', complained of the harsh attitude of officials at employment exchanges, and condemned the failure to bring 'any element of originality or initiative into the consideration of the problems with which they should be dealing'.

There were considerable elements of political calculation in Lemass's parliamentary rhetoric in these early opposition years. There was a sustained effort to score off a government that 'has been driving the industrial car with its foot on the brake instead of on the accelerator', and that had, in Lemass's view, no positive policy to offer.[36] Similarly, he tried to poach from the Labour Party's natural sources of support by presenting Fianna Fáil as more radical than deputies who 'so long as they cannot be accused of being even pale pink in politics seem to think they have fulfilled their functions towards the Irish people'. However, there was also a definite indication of Lemass's own deepest sense of political identity in the deliberate way he challenged and linked the conservatism of agricultural Ireland against the claims of the urban poor. 'I am not, never have been, and probably never will be, a farmer', he told the Dáil, arguing that emigration represented 'the fruits of the policy of allowing the farmers to do what they liked with the land, regardless of its effects upon the community'. Again, he placed it on the record: 'I represent Dublin, and I feel justified in speaking especially about the position in Dublin because of the fact that unemployment in Dublin is worse than in any other part of the state.' Finally, he argued that the two interests were not opposed but complementary:

> until the system of using the land is altered so that more employment can be provided on it, and until industries have been started that will give occupation to the surplus population on the land, we are likely to have these periods of depression recurring quite frequently.

Above all, in private as in public, Seán Lemass remained committed to the central value of political independence. He always saw it as the necessary pre-condition for a prosperous, self-reliant Irish nation and, at this stage, was ready to define that nation in unmistakeable terms: 'Ireland, according to the geography I was taught at school, consists of thirty-two coun-

ties.'[37] Yet, even in this early phase of his thinking, he
[32] envisaged reunification as a gradual process and advocated a
pragmatic approach. Thus he argued for increased pensions on
the grounds that equalisation of social services would help to
'smoothe the path towards the solution of the partition
problem'. Another aspect of his deep nationalist convictions
and Sinn Féin indoctrination was his suspicion of British
motives and his recognition that the interests of the two
islands, although sometimes linked, often diverged. The
explicit anti-British rhetoric of the young Lemass became
more muted in later years but in the early 1930s, as the
country headed towards a general election, he laid on the
nationalism with broad, green strokes.

As the electoral contest came closer, Lemass increased his
already over-loaded schedule. Organisation was as important
as policy formulation if Fianna Fáil were to wrest power and
Lemass was central to both. It required a massive effort, only
ten years after the Treaty debate and six years after the
foundation of the party. Lemass often recalled the exhaustion
mirrored in photographs at the end of the campaign. But the
effort paid handsome dividends. Fianna Fáil with 104
candidates won 44 per cent of the first-preference vote and 72
seats; well ahead of Cumann na nGaedheal's 35 per cent vote
and 56 seats. Lemass's own support dropped by 800 votes but
he again headed the poll, this time over 3,000 votes ahead of
his nearest rival. His period as parliamentary journeyman was
over. Seán Lemass was poised to take office.

3
The Ministerial Tradesman

In 1932 the Department of Industry and Commerce was not the obvious place for Seán Lemass. Although Skinner records it as 'automatic', his own choice would have been Finance and in later years he discussed with de Valera, among others, what effect that appointment might have had on the development of public policy. That speculation could scarcely be more interesting than what actually happened. Lemass took over a department which was not highly regarded; he himself had been a constant, even carping, critic of its policies. The two previous ministers, Joseph McGrath and Patrick McGilligan, had devoted much of their energy to other aspects of public affairs; the latter clearly regarded his other portfolio of External Affairs to be of primary importance. Morale was not high; Lemass found that 'the Department was rotting through inaction'.[1] But the potential was there to convert an administrative backwater into the mainstream of government. The umbrella title Industry and Commerce then sheltered responsibilities nowadays spread over a number of departments, including Social Welfare, Transport and Power, Labour and Energy.

Lemass wasted no time on regrets for what might have been. Nor did he concern himself unduly with the apprehensions of his inherited civil servants. One of his first decisions was to appoint an outsider as Secretary. That man was John Leydon. The appointment created a unique bond between Minister and Secretary; a partnership which 'proved among the most formidable of its kind in the history of the state'.[2] Yet it was an unlikely alliance.

Leydon was a career civil servant whose abilities quickly attracted attention from the mandarins of the new Irish service.

He became a Finance man. Involved in both the all-party
Economic Committee and the Tariff Commission, he must
have been known to Lemass as one of that group of senior
civil servants 'strongly against anything approximating to a
comprehensive system of protection'.[3] His views were
certainly known to the President of the Executive Council,
W. T. Cosgrave, who approached Leydon after the 1932
election to invite him to become Secretary of the Department
of Industry and Commerce. With impeccable propriety,
Leydon declined on the grounds that the appointment might
be unacceptable to the incoming government. When, in turn,
Lemass renewed that offer, Leydon took the trouble to
indicate that he did not agree with the policies and ideas
expressed in Lemass's speeches. The young minister replied
brusquely that he was not looking for a 'yes-man' and would
be prepared to accept reasonable argued advice. Leydon took
the job and together the two men created a dynamic department that was to become a force in the Irish public service
challenging the hegemony of Finance.

The first task was to get the department itself into shape.
In measure Leydon had been chosen because only an
outsider could hope to ride roughshod over the disagreements, personal and professional, which had been allowed
to develop in its senior echelons. Following his minister's
instructions, Leydon called the senior men together and
offered the blunt choice of co-operative working or resignation. There were a few resignations; typically, Lemass
converted what might have been administrative embarrass-
ments into opportunities to create promotions. He quickly
had 'a very good group of officers who could be relied upon
to do very competently anything that had to be done'.[4] But
Lemass had still to secure government sanction for his
chosen policies.

Fianna Fáil had come to office with the support of the
Labour Party, 'pledged to a full-blooded policy of protection
with the stated object of relieving unemployment and of
developing the resources of the country'.[5] All three aspects
were important to Lemass but he was to find it easier to persuade his governmental colleagues to adopt protection than to
take specific action on employment and development policies.

Superficially, his first year in office was an energetic and triumphal progress. Lemass used the Customs Duties (Provisional Imposition) Act and three Finance Acts in May, July and October 1932 to impose duties on a wide range of goods, sometimes following examination of manufacturers' applications, sometimes using his ministerial initiative. Generally British and Commonwealth imports were given a preferential rate until the outbreak of the Economic War led to the Emergency Imposition of Duties Act 1932, which was used to penalise British imports. From now on, protectionism was given an additional patriotic as well as an economic justification. Lemass proved that manufacturers, initially dubious about the policy, could learn to take advantage of it. He also acknowledged to the Dáil that although it was necessary 'to proceed by a system of trial and error . . . protection is given unless facts coerce us to modify them [sic] in some particular way.'[6] The record shows that the weapon of protection, barely invoked previously, became a blunderbuss in the hands of Lemass. He told Michael Mills that it 'was applied in a ruthless way without any clear picture of its merits'. But he did not have everything his own way.

Lemass's first major legislative initiative as Minister was the Control of Manufactures Bill introduced on 8 June 1932 and designed to ensure that Irish industry, now fully protected, should be as far as possible in the hands of Irish citizens and companies. This was to be achieved by requiring new industries to obtain a new manufacture licence and to refuse such licences to non-nationals. A far-reaching measure, it was nevertheless a modified version of Lemass's original draft which 'did not meet with the approval of the cabinet in so far as it applied to the licensing of existing businesses or to businesses owned by citizens of the Free State or by companies a majority of whose share capital is held by citizens of the Free State'; the Minister was instructed to exclude these categories.[7] The fact that this cabinet meeting had lasted nearly six hours is, perhaps, indicative of the degree of difference on policy within the ministerial circle. The original measure itself gives meaning to the informal judgment of a well-placed senior civil servant that Lemass 'was a bit of a dictator'.[8] Despite Lemass's efforts at a further four-hour

long meeting, the government referred the revised draft of
[36] the bill to a two-man committee, consisting of Lemass's old
comrade Tom Derrig, Minister for Education, and one of those
he identified as a cabinet critic, Joseph Connolly, Minister for
Posts and Telegraphs.

It was not the only occasion on which Lemass was reined
in by his colleagues. When he presented proposals for the
reorganisation of the flour-milling industry, the cabinet
response was cool and cautious: 'he was authorised, after
certain modifications, to discuss them tentatively with a
deputation of millers.' But he also scored some notable
successes at the outset of a virtually lifelong struggle with the
Department of Finance.

The first cabinet committee established by the new government was an economic committee. It was given two important
tasks: 'to examine and report to the cabinet on the economic
conditions of the Saorstát' and to prepare 'the necessary
material' for the Imperial Economic Conference in July 1932.
De Valera himself headed the four-man committee. The actual
membership varied, although it must be regarded as amazing
that the Minister for Finance was initially omitted.[9] Subsequently MacEntee and other members of the government
attended meetings and eventually the committee was the
meeting-place for the promised consultations with the Labour
Party deputies. Throughout Lemass was a member.

Despite the absence of the Minister for Finance the early
recommendations of the cabinet economic committee proposed heavy additional expenditure on roads and housing.
The government, of course, approved these and also subsequently authorised Lemass to apply the Trade Loans
(Guarantee) Acts to building schemes, to establish an industrial
development branch in the Department of Industry and
Commerce and to institute a scheme to register the unemployed.
This was undoubtedly a victory over Finance which had
already commented that government commitments would
force a budget deficit:

The motion 'That steps should be taken forthwith by the
executive council to provide work or maintenance to meet
the immediate needs of the unemployed' has been accepted

by the government. It involves commitments of unknown
magnitude for the exchequer. [37]

But administrative inertia and financial caution were not so
easily defeated and Lemass had to adopt some unorthodox
means to win the ensuing debate within the government.

Meantime, he had his first experience representing Ireland
abroad when he accompanied Seán T. O'Kelly, Dr James
Ryan and a twenty-man delegation to the Ottawa Conference.
Again it was noticeable that the Minister for Finance was not
included in a team that included senior officials of his department. The conference was designed to develop the Commonwealth as a free trade area. It had no effect on the deteriorating
Anglo-Irish situation induced by the Economic War, which was
provoked when de Valera, in breach of the Treaty, withheld
land annuities due to Britain. Lemass was happy to join with
others in opposing the British scheme to develop a Commonwealth secretariat. Although he was subsequently to establish
good relations with British ministers Lemass came away from
this first meeting with his prejudices confirmed, more
especially since the British representatives clearly indicated
that they regarded the Fianna Fáil government as temporary.
Before the end of the year, Lemass was arguing in the Senate
that 'the only justification for continuation of the association
with the British Commonwealth was that substantial benefits
were conferred upon the people and, if, as at present, no such
benefits were experienced, then the necessity for maintaining
the association is removed.'[10]

But, more importantly, Lemass was locked in a struggle
with cabinet colleagues and the civil service machine to implement the more radical social and economic policies that he
favoured. Lemass's immediate reaction to the British imposition of tariffs had been to recommend counter-action; he
wrote to de Valera from Ottawa that this turn of events could
work to Ireland's advantage if handled properly and if the
people were prepared to accept the transition. Now he was
again pressing the case for seeing a bleak situation in terms of
opportunity.[11] The Economic War had already had a savage
effect on the Irish economy and on 1 November 1932, in a
'strictly confidential' memorandum to the executive council,

[38] Lemass spelled out the rapid deterioration in the balance of trade and proposed a powerful board to control external trade, under the Department of Industry and Commerce. A week later, in a further memorandum prepared for de Valera, Lemass put forward even more revolutionary proposals for reorganisation based on the assumption that the dispute on repayment of annuities could not be settled. He argued that 'We must plan on this basis' with vehemence, and painted a 'very black picture ... we have reached the point where a collapse of our economic system is in sight.' His solution was a wide-ranging series of proposals to reduce agricultural production, remove people from the land, curtail agricultural profits, create a major public works scheme, expedite industrial developments, reduce imports, establish industrial and agricultural marketing organisations, abolish land annuities, found a state bank and divorce Irish currency from sterling. Lemass admitted that these solutions 'would certainly require dictatorial powers for their execution'. They may well have represented a certain authoritarian radicalism in Lemass's thinking already articulated in his opposition years; they may have been a calculated effort to galvanise the government machine into action. They may also have been a calculated effort to impress the Labour deputies — whose votes were vital to the government's continued survival — with the radicalism of Fianna Fáil policies. They were certain to be resisted.

By now Lemass knew from bitter experience that translating government intention into positive results required both clarity and decision and political will. He also recognised that de Valera was the key. Frustrated in his efforts to alleviate unemployment, he sent a memorandum to the President of the Executive Council with an accompanying personal letter on 14 November 1932:

A Chara,
We have frequently discussed the steps that must be taken to provide for the unemployed and have, more or less, accepted responsibility for giving effect to the principle of 'work or maintenance' in so far as it may be practical to do so. Our discussions have, however, been confined, up to the present, to the public works which could be initiated,

due, no doubt, to a natural inclination to deal with unemployment by the provision of work rather than by maintenance allowances. These discussions have, nevertheless, made it very clear that with existing machinery, it is not possible to deal with the great mass of unemployed even if the finances and schemes of work were available, which, as we know, is not the case. It is equally clear that a considerable time must elapse before the examination of the financial problems involved can be completed and also that large scale public works will take an equally long time to get going. In the meantime, the unemployed are there, dependent on what they can get from the Home Assistance Funds and private charities, which is altogether inadequate. In these circumstances, something more than relief schemes on the scale on which they can now be undertaken is required.

I have two definite proposals to put which, if adopted, will cope adequately with the situation, in my opinion. I am putting them in this personal way rather than through my department because I am not clear that the initiation of proposals of this character is my official responsibility and from the nature of the proposals you will see that other departments are directly involved. I think, therefore, that it is preferable that you should bring them up for consideration by the council, if you can.[12]

The two definite proposals were: legislation to protect lower-income bona fide unemployed from eviction for non-payment of rent; and the provision of weekly unemployment assistance, subject to a means test.

The letter reveals some enduring characteristics of Lemass's political aims, style and methods: the impatience to short-circuit discussion and procedure, the demand for decision and action, the recognition, to adapt Truman's phrase, that the buck starts with the head of government. The outcome shows how cautiously and slowly the Irish system operates. Lemass's attempt to curb property rights was rejected by the economic committee. His unemployment scheme was sent to a committee of officials on 18 November 1932; their interim report the following February saw 'no prospect of immediate relief for those whom the scheme is designed to assist'. A final report and Lemass's criticism were circulated in May and the Minister authorised to draw up a bill in June which was introduced to the Dáil in August 1933.[13] In December 1932, the cabinet also shelved Lemass's wide-ranging scheme for national reorganisation; some proposals were rejected, others withdrawn or deferred.

By now Lemass, like other members of the cabinet, was more immediately concerned with the short-term survival of Fianna Fáil in power than with long-term planning. Dependence on Labour had become increasingly irksome and uncertain; the attempt to keep the two parties in tandem through weekly meetings had broken down. According to Lemass's recollection, de Valera telephoned to tell him that Labour would vote against proposed government cuts in civil service salaries and asked what he would do. Lemass did not hesitate: 'I'd dissolve the Dáil before they got a chance of voting and have another election.'[14] According to others, de Valera's decision was taken alone and was a great surprise to his ministers. An alert contemporary political observer described it as 'a master stroke of strategy'. Whatever the circumstances of the decision, the effect was to plunge the party into another whirlwind campaign.

Seán Lemass served again as director of elections. Fianna Fáil consolidated its position as the major Irish political party, gaining nearly 50 per cent of the first-preference vote (19 per cent ahead of Cumann na nGaedheal) and for the first time winning an overall majority. Lemass's own contribution to the growth of the party in these formative years is reflected in the steady increase in the Fianna Fáil vote in Dublin city over four general elections:

Fianna Fáil percentage of first-preference vote in four general elections

	June 1927	Sept. 1927	1932	1933
Dublin North	22	25	35	45
Dublin South	29	35	41	53

His continuing personal electoral appeal was again reflected in the 1933 result. He gained more than 4,000 extra votes to head the poll, over 6,000 votes ahead of his nearest rival. It was a remarkable achievement for a young man but electoral performance was less important for Lemass than the continuing fight to implement his chosen policies in government.

Lemass's public record in the 1930s is a series of political successes. De Valera, of course, dominated the scene. The major constitutional and Anglo-Irish clashes of the period suggest an Ireland still in an earlier phase of its historical development. But the country was changing as protection replaced free trade, and Lemass was careful to insist that his measures were not reactions to the circumstances of the Economic War but were 'primarily designed to provide more effective machinery to develop the industrial activities and the industrial potentialities of this country.' The scope of this 'machinery' is reflected in the bills, licences, orders that emanated from Lemass's office.

The most enduring monuments, perhaps, were the creation of a whole population of state-promoted companies; they included the Industrial Credit Company, Bórd na Móna, Aer Lingus, the Irish Life Assurance Board, Industrial Alcohol Factories Ltd, and the Irish Tourist Board. Lemass was involved in efforts to sustain and develop the ESB, the railways, and the Irish Sugar Company. His Cement Act 1933 was pushed through in the face of internal and external opposition. The story of these companies illuminates many facets of Lemass's career, not least a consistent ambition to convert the Irish public service into a fountainhead for entrepreneurial development corporations. They show the pragmatic character of his economic thinking; the willingness to substitute state enterprise when private initiative was lacking. Perhaps, above all, they underline Lemass's determination to force through his own policy preferences. An episode is reported in his protracted campaign to engage a reluctant ESB in turf-fired generating stations.[15] Having already manoeuvred the ESB into technical comments that virtually committed them to turf, he 'exercised a skilful combination of controlled loss of temper and reasonableness' to force them to action. An internal ESB minute catches the tone of a stormy interview between the young Minister and the ESB's chairman and chief design engineer:

> The Minister stated that his letter was an 'ultimatum' and apparently it was not being taken as such by the Board. The government was placing 'a brick wall around this country' and Irish fuel had to be used. Comparisons with the use of imported fuels did not arise, and if any future proposals were received by him for a plant utilising imported fuels 'there would be a devil of a row'. The Minister further stressed that any failure on the part of the collieries, the Turf Board or his own department would not be accepted as an alibi for the Board.

But episodes such as this, and less stormy relations between the Minister and the widening range of state companies, represented only one part of Lemass's impact on public policy.

He was also involved in welfare legislation, ranging from unemployment assistance through to children's allowances, which required all his persuasive efforts. Already in 1937 when he became President of the International Labour Office Conference in Geneva, he could be proposed as 'the author of comprehensive measures, reducing hours of labour, extending special protection to women and young persons, and encouraging the practice of collective bargaining . . . young in years, but already long experienced in the art of government'.[16] Above all, he was seen as the engineer of protectionist policies which by the end of 1937 were calculated to be subjecting nearly 2,000 articles to restriction or control. The web of Industry and Commerce reached out to every aspect of Irish industrial and commercial life and Lemass was the target of more parliamentary questions than any other minister. It says much for his capacity and growing assurance that he was able to cope with this work load and be marked as an outstanding success.

Lemass's public political success was not earned without constant private effort. Some within the government, many within the public service, doubted the wisdom of such radical action without mature consideration. He did not win all his cabinet battles: for example, additional names were added to his proposed nominees to the Industrial Research Council, his attempt to exempt the industrial alcohol factories from rates was denied, and his effort to lower the level for means testing was rejected.[17] Above all, from the beginning, there was a constant tension with the Department of Finance and its Minister, Seán MacEntee. Some instances of these 'repeated differences' are recorded in Fanning's authoritative history of that department. Dr Fanning commented that 'likelihood of policy differences between the two departments was accentuated because of the characters of those in charge in Industry and Commerce.'[18] But Lemass's tone in exchange with other cabinet colleagues was not calculated to encourage warm relationships. He was assertive in discussion and sharp in written criticism. One example in his comment on a scheme by Frank Aiken for a new volunteer force in the army: 'It is not clear from the documents circulated what scheme the Minister is now proposing to the council . . . I do not think either scheme conforms to the decisions made by the cabinet committee as I understand them.' Another was his insistent argument that no proper policy on agricultural production could be developed until a firm and clear decision was made on the major priority.

Some colleagues fought back. On occasions they tried to use Lemass's own tactic of direct appeal to de Valera to curtail their colleague's conduct of affairs. But, as his biographers comment:

> de Valera, who was well able to practice judicious delegation, respected Lemass's preference for a large degree of autonomy. He gave his able Minister for Industry and Commerce confidence and support, in full measure, which were invaluable throughout the years, particularly whenever doubts and reservations occured on the part of other members of the government. Yet the outlook of the two men on economic and social matters was not identical.

And cabinet colleagues drew attention, as did later critics, to Lemass's indifference to regional economic imbalance. In 1935, the issue was Gaeltacht industries; in 1964, it was the national wage agreement. In both cases, the outcome was to reinforce Lemass's position and influence.[19]

On 27 February 1935, Senator Joseph Connolly, Minister
[44] for Lands, complained to the executive council:

> There is growing impatience with the government's so-called
> neglect of the Gaeltacht areas with regard to industrial
> development. This has been expressed at party meetings
> by deputies representing Gaeltacht constituencies and was,
> I understand, the subject of a resolution at the Fianna Fáil
> executive. It is consistently expressed to me in correspond-
> ence and meetings which I have attended in Connemara,
> West Cork, Donegal and elsewhere in the Gaeltacht ...
> The policy of industrial development is entirely one for the
> Minister of Industry and Commerce and in directing and
> influencing manufacturing concerns the Minister, will, no
> doubt, experience difficulty in inducing them to ignore the
> eastern seaboard or the larger ports. ... Nevertheless, we
> have, I feel, reached the position when we must decide
> whether we mean to do anything to provide employment in
> the Gaeltacht areas or if our policy is one of acceptance
> of the idea that it is neither practical nor advisable to direct
> or divert certain industries to those areas.

The topic was one close to de Valera's own most cherished
ideals. The challenge to Lemass's policy emphasis was direct
and unequivocal. Lemass's response was blunt and brutal:
the only solution to the social and economic problems of the
Gaeltacht would involve a co-ordinated plan to reduce
population congestion and induce young people to migrate
through special training and school schemes, labour camps
and special Gaeltacht recruitment into industry, the army and
gardaí. Lemass also proposed the abolition of rates and taxes,
an experimental turf-fired generating station in Donegal and
that the Gaeltacht industries section of the Department of
Lands be replaced by a special board. It was a radical solution,
social surgery that might well have killed the economically
ailing Gaeltacht patient. In fact virtually nothing was done; a
later schedule lists twenty-nine proposals by Lands for the
benefit of the Gaeltacht between 1932 and 1937 turned down
by other departments, in eighteen cases by Industry and
Commerce.[20] Lemass found Connolly a difficult colleague
and, whether that view was shared, after the abolition of the

Irish Free State Senate in 1936, he ceased to be a member of the government.

The mid-thirties were a busy time for the de Valera government. Abolition of the Senate was only one part of a package of major political changes that spanned the removal of the oath through to the creation of a new Constitution. Lemass seems to have paid little close attention to these developments. He was content to follow de Valera's lead. This is revealed in relation to the drafting of the Constitution.[21] A pencilled note indicates that the Department of Industry and Commerce, usually prompt in offering opinions, had made no observations on the first official draft circulated. Subsequently, Lemass did have a personal correspondence with de Valera suggesting some detailed modifications in the wording of the 'Directive Principles of Social Policy' which became Article 45 of the Constitution. He also enclosed Leydon's observations. The main purpose seems to have been to tone down the language. Perhaps it is best explained in the reported words attributed to Lemass by de Valera's official biographers: 'You know, Chief', he said, 'we can't very well make the Constitution a manifesto of Fianna Fáil policy.' In fact, the suggested modifications, incorporated in the final text, are more precise than this account might suggest. But Lemass's real interests were elsewhere: in pressing ahead with his own policies for economic development, continuing as a major spokesman for the government in the Dáil and remaining active in ensuring the smooth running of the party organisation.

The election of 1937 was combined with a national referendum on adoption of the new Constitution. While the Constitution was supported by over 56 per cent of the voters, backing for Fianna Fáil slipped to 45 per cent. In a smaller Dáil the government lost eight seats and its overall majority. Fianna Fáil formed a new government with Labour support but an early election could now be expected. That was an additional responsibility to be shouldered.

With so much to do, even for a man with his remarkable energy, Lemass had little time for private life.[22] Rearing the growing family was largely left to his wife. The children often saw almost as much of his official drivers as of their father. They were surrogate uncles who could fix bikes and mend toys. In 1934, the family had moved from Rathgar to [46] Churchtown Park in Dundrum; four years later they moved again to Palmerston Road. The houses were close enough to his work to allow Lemass home for lunch some days. That was one break in a day spent between the office in Industry and Commerce, Leinster House, Government Buildings and a variety of party and public functions. Apart from a round of golf and card games, which became an exaggerated Lemass legend, only the family holiday and evenings spent in the company of close friends offered relaxation. In these busy years, the renditions of his favoured party-piece, 'Dangerous Dan McGrew' or occasional music-hall songs became less frequent. Seán Lemass sacrificed leisure to work; he was the epitome of the professional, full-time politician. Mrs Lemass has sketched the routine:

> From the day he entered the Dáil, a suitcase had to be ready. Seán was forever trotting around the country trying to build up the Fianna Fáil organisation and during by-elections he hardly slept at all. . . . He used to breakfast in bed at 8.00 a.m. and carefully read all the morning newspapers. By 9.30 a.m. he was in his office at Leinster House. Although there was nothing he liked better than to relax by the fire with me and the children, he rarely got the opportunity.
> Sometimes Dáil business could keep him away until after midnight. Then there were at least five or six functions a week which he felt we had to attend. He used to say to me that our lives were not our own in politics.
> Even when we used to take a house in Skerries for the summer months, Seán never joined us until night time and even then he usually carried a briefcase full of business with him. When we did get a chance to relax, we either played poker or he read historical biographies.

He played cards, even in the family, as he played politics — to win; he disliked chatter interrupting play. He also enjoyed occasional light fiction. The Lemass children often found him distant rather than strict; keen that they should get the benefit of education without being insistent. At home he was a man of his time: conventionally attached to middle-class

respectability, easily upset by domestic crises, willing to
relinquish responsibility to his wife:

> He would say to me, 'Kathleen, you will have to cope with
> the home for the moment. I have to cope with the country.'

And, as war approached, there were ample problems to be
faced.

The administrative process of preparing the Irish economy
for war conditions began in 1938. But there were four other
major issues that claimed Lemass's attention in that year: the
trade talks with Britain between January and April; the report
of the Banking Commission published in March; the general
election campaign in May-June and the struggle to provide an
independent source of petrol supply, long debated within the
government, which surfaced in the Dáil in July.

In the preliminary talks that preceded the formal opening
of renewed negotiations with Britain, de Valera had made it
clear 'that discussions by civil servants would be of no use,
as the questions were essentially ones which would have to be
decided by principals'.[23] His priorities for discussion were:
partition, defence, finance and trade; the over-riding British
concern was political. The Irish team, approved at a cabinet
meeting of 7 January 1938, consisted of de Valera, MacEntee
(Finance), Ryan (Agriculture) and Seán Lemass. Lemass's
recollection was that de Valera mainly conducted the formal
negotiations; if other members of the Irish delegation had
comments to make they were written down and passed to him.
As far as detailed trade negotiations were concerned, the Irish,
he recalled, were in a stronger position than the British. It was
a unique experience. Britain desired a settlement; Lemass's
task was to extract the maximum benefit. In this effort,
Leydon's personal contacts with Whitehall officials were
invaluable in heading off a British effort to regain control over
Irish tariffs on their goods. In the end, the agreement
guaranteed free entry to the British market for Irish industrial
goods (with a few insignificant exceptions), the Irish right to
maintain protective tariffs, while securing equal market access
for Irish as for British farmers. In a sense, it was a one-way free
trade agreement in Ireland's favour but it was a successful
end to the Economic War. It was not the final settlement

of partition desired by de Valera, but it represented for
[48] Lemass a real opportunity for Irish economic growth.

The majority report of the Banking Commission was critical of the expansionist and interventionist policies associated with Lemass.[24] Since his years in opposition, he had been critical of the banking system; in the Dáil in 1931 he had advocated the establishment of a proper central bank in Dublin and the creation of an independent currency to save Ireland from the effects of the British financial crisis. In their first years in government the Fianna Fáil ministers debated vigorously what should be done about financial policy and the banking system. Aiken was interested in monetary reform. MacEntee, despite his colourful opposition rhetoric, was in reality a conservative. De Valera was prepared to move, if necessary, to alleviate the twin problems of emigration and unemployment. Lemass, in the words of the best-informed and best-placed observer,

> approached these matters, as he approached most others, with a keen practical mind and a readiness to explore new ways and to take what he possibly would have described as 'calculated risks'.[25]

Action was deferred pending the recommendations of the Banking Commission, suggested by MacEntee. Lemass was not enthusiastic about the Commission and with other ministers opposed its establishment. He later recalled his disillusionment at the deferential attitude adopted by Irish representatives to their international consultants. At a dinner, he observed that Brennan and McElligott, the mandarins of Finance, treated Per Jacobsson as though he were an economic pope. Lemass did not feel competent enough to argue against banking conservatism at this level. In cabinet he had no inhibitions. The majority report of the Banking Commission recommended the retention of parity with sterling, a new Currency Commission to act as a central bank with very limited powers, tight control on borrowing by semi-state organisations and careful examination of 'various government proposals with more regard to their possible monetary and financial reactions'. Fundamentally, the recommended conservative recipe was to leave things as they were. That was not Lemass's way. There were three minority reports submitted and the fact that de Valera favoured one of these made it easier for Lemass to oppose the conservative orthodoxy of the majority report. Certainly, the recommendations appear to have had little real influence on either government policy or public discussion although, to Lemass's annoyance, Finance continued to use the Banking Commission's arguments in attempts to obstruct his policies. There was also a long war of attrition by Finance against Lemass's efforts to establish an Irish central bank with real powers to control currency credit and investment.

Meantime he was involved in another general election campaign. On 25 July 1938, the opposition unexpectedly forced a division on a technical aspect of an arbitration scheme for civil service salaries; Labour joined Fine Gael in the lobbies and the government was defeated by a single vote. De Valera promptly went to the country. There was little mood for change in Ireland; Fianna Fáil could claim credit for an agreement which restored the ports and ended the Economic War. The outcome was a triumph. For the first time the party secured an absolute majority of the first-preference vote and 72 of the 138 seats. Lemass's personal vote slipped back but he again secured more than two quotas and more than double the vote of the nearest rival candidate. It was a remarkable electoral achievement for a man who had little time, or indeed inclination, for the normal round of personal nursing demanded by Irish constituency politics. It marked another aspect of his consummate skill as a politician.

Lemass had less success in his efforts to develop Irish oil refining capacity.[26] The question was touched on in a stormy debate on the transfer of control for the industrial alcohol factories. Less publicly the issue had been contentious for years. As early as April 1931 the Department had put forward a project to grant a monopoly to an Irish-based refining company; this had been rejected. Lemass as Minister had pressed forward with a similar scheme in 1935 but had been stubbornly opposed by the Department of Finance, who complained both about the lack of consultation and the details of the proposed arrangements in terms of cost, quality of product and viability. The Attorney-General expressed reservations: 'I have no desire to hamper the Minister for Industry and Commerce . . . loosely worded agreements how-

ever are the source of endless trouble.' So did a strongly
[50] worded memorandum from Lemass's old adversary Senator
Connolly: 'The Minister for Lands feels that the whole plan
and scheme is unsatisfactory from the point of view of
national economic interest.' MacEntee wrote directly to
de Valera a three-page letter: 'I feel very grave doubts indeed
as to whether in their present form the proposals are equitable
to our people. . . . I think they are too greedy. . . . I put these
views before you as I think that in all the circumstances I
ought not to take part in the further discussions.' Despite
these internal cabinet objections, Lemass was eventually
authorised to make an agreement with a British company, the
London and Thames Oil Water Co., and work began on the oil
refinery site at the North Wall. But the battleground had
shifted from the cabinet room in Dublin where Lemass
wielded power to the commercial world of London where he
had no influence. British oil interests, especially the Shell
company, had been openly hostile to any projected Irish
refinery and forced the original contractor to withdraw.
Lemass then secured a new partner in the project, the shipping
magnate Andrew Weir, who was prepared to take on the oil
interests and undertook to provide a fleet of oil tankers. But,
by now, with war imminent, the oil refinery project had to be
shelved and Lemass was increasingly concerned with his new
responsibilities as Minister for Supplies. If his first seven years
in Industry and Commerce had proved him an energetic,
skilful and innovative ministerial tradesman, the next phase of
his career showed his capacity to practice his craft in a
different and larger context.

4
The Mature Ministerial Craftsman

The Supplies Episode[1]

The Irish administrative machine had begun making preparations to organise for a major international emergency since the mid-thirties. Between 1935 and 1938, a secret inter-departmental committee of civil servants had prepared a series of three reports on basic supplies: fuel and oil; cereals, animal foodstuffs, salt, sugar and tea; foodstuffs, seeds, fertilisers, tobacco and drink. In August 1938, the committee recommended that additional progress required a different form of organisation with full-time officers. On 7 September, an assistant secretary and other staff from the Department of Industry and Commerce were assigned to form a separate emergency supplies branch. This was the nucleus of what, twelve months later, became the Department of Supplies with Seán Lemass in charge. The original branch began by surveying the principal Irish trades and industries and held discussions with a variety of business organisations and prominent individuals to encourage them to prepare for an emergency. The main emphasis was on securing and building up supplies.

Generally the response from business was positive and co-operative; although many importers were reluctant to believe that Britain would ever consider, let alone find it necessary, to prohibit the export of essential supplies to Ireland. Some areas acted more promptly than others. The flour millers set up a special wheat reserve committee to co-ordinate increased imports of wheat. But the oil distributors, although pressed from September 1938 onwards, did little to develop extra reserves; probably, as the record notes,

'due in some measure to their disgruntlement over the negotiations to establish an oil refinery in Dublin'. Later on, during
the war, Lemass was to have further experiences of the willingness and capacity of British-based oil interests to play politics
and frustrate his plans.

[52]

Lemass also had to overcome resistance from financial
interests. In January 1939, the Federation of Irish Manufacturers pointed out that most of their members, while
anxious to support the national effort, could not afford to
finance large-scale purchase of additional stocks; they asked
for government credits at reasonable rates of interest. Various
possible methods of direct state interventions were considered
but it was finally decided that the ordinary commercial banks
should provide the necessary credit. The banks were not
enthusiastic and it required direct official representation with
the Irish Banks' Standing Committee to secure additional
funding for these extra stocks; they did not reduce the rate
of interest; they refused the request for a preferential rate. The
comment in the Department of Supplies' 'Historical Survey'
reflects Lemass's judgment on the Irish banking community:

> the Irish banks who, in 1938/39, would not advance money
> at 4 per cent to an Irish manufacturer for the purchase of
> raw materials, were at a later date prepared to gamble it
> for a mere 2 per cent on the survival of the British empire
> by investing in British loans.[2]

Insuring property and goods against war risks was another
problem tackled by Lemass. It was to drag on throughout the
war and Lemass had to invoke de Valera's own authority to
force action from the Department of Finance. The issue was
first raised by Industry and Commerce in October 1938. Five
months later, Finance replied that any insurance scheme
would be regarded as 'additional taxation' and suggested the
matter be postponed and a possible scheme of compensation
be considered at the end of the war. In July 1939, Lemass
threw his weight behind an unorthodox proposal by Leydon
to accept the offer of re-insurance for Irish ships from the
British Board of Trade. Intensive pressure by Lemass brought
agreement from MacEntee and, on the same afternoon, 'after
some hesitation', from de Valera. However, the Finance stone-

walling on a general war risk insurance scheme remained firm.

As such issues surfaced more frequently in 1939 and the course of international developments brought war closer, the case for a major re-organisation of governmental functions and priorities became more urgent. It was also increasingly evident, as Leydon reported on 1 May following one of his many visits to London in this period, that it was time to regularise arrangements for securing supplies; informal assurances by British civil servants should be replaced by 'an agreement between the two governments.'[3] But it was only with the actual outbreak of war that de Valera bowed to the inevitable, regrouped his cabinet and created a new Department of Supplies. Lemass's virtually automatic appointment marked a heightened plateau in his ministerial career. More than anything he had yet achieved, this episode in Supplies set the public seal of approval on his growing reputation as the most formidable ministerial craftsman of his generation. It enabled him to extend even further his already considerable influence on both the formulation and application of the government's economic policy. He became responsible, in de Valera's own words, for the 'central planning department for our economic life'. It was a powerful strategic position; Lemass was determined to use it.

De Valera's particular trust in and dependence on Lemass was marked. In his speech on the critically important Emergency Powers Bill, the Taoiseach told the Dáil that Lemass 'will take charge of the bill in the House, and if there are any particular questions which arise as regards the general application of any of those sections, he will give you answer and reason as to why those powers are necessary'. That was a direct endorsement.

More indirectly, Lemass's influence with de Valera can be measured in the allocation of ministerial offices within the new cabinet. It was the most extensive reshuffle in the history of the independent Irish state; a major shift in the internal balance of power, both in organisational and personnel terms. Two new posts were created: Lemass taking over Supplies, Frank Aiken becoming Minister for the Co-ordination of Defensive Measures. Seán MacEntee was shifted to Industry and Commerce, and Finance was taken over by the Tanaiste, Seán T. O'Kelly. His vacancy in Local Government was filled

by moving Paddy Ruttledge from Justice and putting Gerry
[54] Boland in his place. The consequent vacancy in Lands was
filled by Tom Derrig (who also served briefly in Posts and
Telegraphs until P. J. Little was promoted to the post from
chief whip). Oscar Traynor became Minister for Defence
and de Valera added Education to his existing responsibilities
as Taoiseach and Minister for External Affairs. Dr James
Ryan in Agriculture was the only minister to retain his existing portfolio. It would be difficult to exaggerate the predominance of Lemass's new department. Supplies, in
Dr Fanning's considered verdict,

> played the key role of directing the supply and distribution
> of agricultural and of manufactured products. As such, it
> was responsible for co-ordinating and, in practice, directing
> many of the activities of two other major government
> departments — Agriculture and Industry and Commerce . . .
> [it] inevitably usurped certain Finance prerogatives, hitherto
> undisputed.

The reshuffle provided ample opportunity for the opposition. The matter was first raised by W. T. Cosgrave in a
parliamentary question. De Valera, in a brief reply, said that
'no change of policy is involved, as may be realised from the
fact the reallocation which has been made does not involve
any change in the personnel of the government as a whole.'[4]
That answer was unlikely to satisfy anyone. In the subsequent
three-day adjournment debate, Fine Gael and Labour deputies
repeatedly speculated about the real purposes of the changes;
they rehearsed rumours ranging from the shrewd to the
bizarre. Generally, they concentrated their attack on two
points: that a wholesale reshuffle was unwise in a time of
emergency and that the replacement of the Minister for
Finance in particular required explanation. Cosgrave complained that he had not been given a fair answer to his
parliamentary question and that the transfer of Lemass to
Supplies had apparently caused six other changes, including
the Minister for Finance who 'is either promoted or demoted'.
Both Richard Corish of Labour and Fine Gael deputy, J.
Hurley, mentioned rumours that the change in Finance was
designed to put in a Minister who 'favours a change in the

currency'. P. McGilligan argued that this particular change has caused 'the greatest possible disquiet'. T. O'Higgins criticised [55] the whole reorganisation with the dismissive argument that 'an experienced dud is better than an inexperienced dud'. De Valera attempted to brush aside the opposition charges of cabinet dissension: 'we are a very united family.' He gave an elaborate explanation for the various changes. In particular, de Valera justified the transfer of MacEntee to Industry and Commerce on the grounds that:

> I thought the best person to fill the vacancy was the person who had been most intimately in touch with the Minister for that Department, as the Minister for Finance is with practically every Department and particularly with the Department of Industry and Commerce. There is a number of things with regard to which he [MacEntee] had to have contact with the Minister for Industry and Commerce over a long period, and I thought that the best person to put in as Minister for Industry and Commerce was the Minister for Finance.

De Valera's explanation for the whole reshuffle is scarcely convincing. Certainly the reference to the contact between Lemass and MacEntee was disingenuous. The two had frequently disagreed on policy. Their disagreements went beyond the anticipated institutional tensions between men responsible for such divergent departments of state. There is evidence that relations between the two, never close, had become increasingly strained.

In February 1939, Lemass had closed a personal correspondence with MacEntee with what amounted to a threat. 'It is not reasonable on your part,' he complained, 'to hold up my proposals [on the subject of a flying boat base on the Shannon] for a period of two months . . . if I do not hear from you I propose merely to say that the proposals have been before your department since 13 December last, but that I have not yet received your concurrence.'[5] MacEntee, too, had registered complaints. In a letter to de Valera at the beginning of May 1939 he rejected Lemass's attack on Finance attitudes to the Industrial Credit Corporation as unfair and unjustified; MacEntee pointedly noted that

Lemass's statement that he had personally written to Finance was not 'borne out by records or recollection'. These types of exchange go beyond inter-departmental disputes and reflect deeper differences between the two men. Lemass in later years made no secret of his opposition to what he saw as MacEntee's conservatism; he recalled his irritation with MacEntee as one of the ministers reluctant to spend money on building up supplies.[6] Some well-placed observers have hinted that there was substance in the suggestion, made by a political opponent, that Lemass had refused to continue in government if MacEntee remained in Finance. Certainly Lemass adopted this tactic in the fifties and for the next quarter of a century the two men continued to have disagreements about basic policies. For the moment, through the Department of Supplies, Lemass was placed in a dominant position.

He had virtually unlimited powers to control exports, imports, prices of commodities of all kinds and to regulate 'the treatment, keeping, storage, movement, distribution, sale, purchase, use, and consumption of articles of all kinds,'[7] under the Emergency Powers Act. Lemass lost no time in using these powers: between 1939 and 1943 he made a total of 602 orders. The majority of these were concerned with the rationing of consumer goods, the fixing of prices and the control of production and so affected the whole population or substantial sections of it. In addition, Lemass gave specific directions to particular manufacturers and distributors. He was constantly faced with long lists of parliamentary questions and searching criticisms in the course of Estimate and other Dáil debates. On six separate occasions he delivered ministerial broadcasts on radio dealing with the supply position.

Lemass brought Leydon with him as secretary to the new department. Both men recognised from the beginning that the normal pace and customary caution of the civil service were inappropriate to the circumstances. Innovation and experience, pragmatism and energy fused to produce a uniquely flexible, practical and decisive machine. The Department of Supplies, reflecting the style of its joint masters, placed a high priority on prompt despatch of business. Officers in the department were encouraged to use the telephone in preference to correspondence; internal memoranda were reduced to a minimum.

All representations received by the Department were expected to receive a reply within a week; anything unanswered within a fortnight was raked up and scrutinised at the top.

Lemass inaugurated a departmental cabinet system. Once or twice a week he met in conference with Leydon and the assistant secretaries. These sessions went beyond review and communication; 'decisions were taken on all major questions arising in the course of the day-to-day work of the Department.'[8] In a further effort to cut through red tape, Lemass reached further down the administrative hierarchy and from July 1943 onwards he involved principal officers from relevant sections in these conferences. His experience with these procedures in Supplies encouraged him to adopt similar conferences on his return to Industry and Commerce, and undoubtedly influenced his handling of government business when he became Taoiseach. This period in Supplies sharpened and deepened his initial conviction that the main function of the government minister was to take decisions. In a typical reply to a written question on the relationship of minister and civil service, he later answered:

> The end of every investigation or study carried out in a government should be a ministerial or government decision. I think it was John Fitzgerald Kennedy who said that the function of the civil service expert was to examine a question to a conclusion, while the function of the political head of his department was to examine it to a decision. Whether in the formulation of new policies or the fulfilment of older ones, the mainspring of activity in every department of government is the ministerial decision. On the minister's capacity to give speedy and clear decisions on matters coming up to him from the department and also on the extent to which the understanding of the minister's aims permeates all its activities depends the effectiveness of every department. In the same way, new ideas emerging from departmental studies make no progress until the minister gives them his endorsement and support.

Lemass's emphasis on decision was paramount in Supplies. He was prepared to acknowledge, even to anticipate, that mistakes would be made. While constant efforts to consult affected interests were encouraged and fostered, this was not always possible. Lemass preferred to act decisively and adjust subsequently rather than postpone choice pending complete investigation. The strategy is noted in the 'Historical Survey' of the Department of Supplies:

> During the emergency period serious problems often arose which had to be solved immediately. . . . It became the accepted policy that it was better . . . to take some action quickly (even if later experience was to suggest modifications) than to attempt to find the perfect solution by waiting until all the facts had been ascertained . . . ad hoc schemes for distribution and tentative solutions of problems adopted at an early stage had often to be altered. Nevertheless, experience showed that the policy was a wise one and that the surest way of finding the flaws in any scheme was to put it in operation.

This unorthodox approach to public administration often attracted parliamentary criticism. Lemass had little difficulty in justifying his policies in the light of emergency circumstances. But this period in Supplies may well have encouraged a certain cavalier attitude to orderly processes of decision-making (already evident in applying protection) which marked Lemass's later career. It certainly exhibited the energetic pragmatism which was his most constant characteristic.

Faced with the problem of producing a nationwide supply of individual ration books, Lemass went outside the civil service machine. Originally, in opposition, he had not approved of the licensing of the Hospitals' Trust Sweepstakes; in office, he had become persuaded that the scheme had positive benefits. Now he used their apparatus to solve an emergency dilemma and awarded the Sweepstakes a £17,000 contract to write up ration books in eight weeks. Similarly, redundant ESB staff were seconded to fill temporary posts in the Department of Supplies; and Customs and Excise men, whose normal duties had fallen off, were recruited to staff the inspection branch.

As the war lengthened, the supply situation deteriorated. The black market offered opportunities for quick profit; those given privileged supplies were not always scrupulous in their use. Lemass took a severe line with offenders. He pressed the argument that in such cases above all, justice must be seen to be done; that the public would accept a considerable degree of unavoidable hardship if schemes were recognised to be fair and equitable. He was relentless in pursuing offenders, and, after a struggle, managed to speed up prosecutions. On occasions, despite some protests, rationing offences were dealt with in the special court. Lemass took a certain grim satisfaction in the fact that acquaintances of his own were prosecuted. He was no respecter of reputations and vigorously defended his department's determination to stamp out irregularities.[9] Apart from irregularities dealt with by way of warnings, nearly 5,000 prosecutions were instituted in three years, 1941-3, and convictions obtained in 85 per cent of these cases. Despite the temptations and opportunities to which they were exposed, only two officials of his department were found to be involved in issuing unauthorised documents.

Perhaps because of the equity and efficiency with which the problems of rationing were handled, Lemass avoided the public odium that might be expected to attach to the 'Minister for Shortages'. Mrs Lemass recalled: 'they used to call him "Half-Ounce Lemass" because of the rationing but he always took that as a joke.'[10] He was also seen to share the deprivations suffered by ordinary citizens: he was pictured arriving at functions on a bicycle and remembered that 'it took a long time for the muscles of my legs to respond to this harsh treatment.'

But his real political skills were seen in the capacity to convert unpleasant necessity to advantage. James Meenan has commented:

> Throughout all vicissitudes, Mr Lemass never hesitated to prepare everybody for the worst. This was superlatively good public relations. The worst never did quite come to the worst; and everybody put up with a lot because they had been prepared to have to put up with so much more. In those years, Mr Lemass consistently concealed the strength of his hand.[11]

Professor Meenan, who has accurately identified Lemass's public relations skill, may have underestimated the real emer-

gencies that arose. Lemass recalled the situation in late 1941
[60] when petrol supplies were almost exhausted. He then received
word that a tanker shipment was due on Christmas Eve and
went home relieved. However, the cargo was too heavy to
allow the tanker clear the bar in Dublin Bay and had to
discharge some of the oil at Liverpool. While there it was sunk
and the value of the petrol coupon had to be cut from two
gallons to a quarter of a gallon. Lemass's own assessment on
this issue is perhaps more realistic: without proper storage
facilities and while subject to submarine attacks on tankers,
petrol supplies were always precarious. Lemass succeeded less
by exaggerating difficulties than by spelling them out clearly
but with the confidence that they could be overcome. He
embodied the national capacity to respond to the challenge.

Lemass developed a number of new state enterprises to
cope with national needs during the emergency. Perhaps the
most important was Irish Shipping – the beginning of that
Irish merchant marine envisaged by Sinn Féin before the First
World War. The Insurance Corporation of Ireland was a
response to exorbitant increases demanded by London
brokers. A range of companies were established to take advantage of joint purchase and importation scheme: these included
Grain Importers (Éire) Ltd; Animal Feeding Stuffs (Éire) Ltd;
Timber Importers Ltd; Fuel Importers Ltd; Tea Importers
Ltd; and Oil and Fats Ltd.

But there were many problems in ensuring supplies, especially as British attitudes towards Irish neutrality became
increasingly negative. Leydon's warning on the inadequacy of
informal arrangements was soon justified. Lemass's own
wariness about dependence on British goodwill – first
expressed back in the 1920s – was confirmed by his war-time
experiences. On 21 March 1940[12] de Valera cautiously raised
the question of possible trade discussions at ministerial level
with the cabinet; the secretary was instructed not to note
these discussions in the minutes. A week later the government
decided that if the talks were to take place they should be
conducted by Lemass and Ryan. It was a very qualified and
tentative approval:

these two ministers will in the first instance conduct dis-

cussions of a general exploratory character and if necessary
the question of Taoiseach subsequently proceeding to [61]
London will be considered in due course.

At the end of April Lemass and Ryan began talks in London.
It soon became apparent that Britain wanted to secure trans-
shipment and storage rights which would compromise Irish
neutrality. There was also a dispute about agricultural prices.
In the event, no new agreement was concluded and with the
nomination of Churchill as prime minister further restrictions
were placed on British supplies to Ireland. One curious feature
of these Anglo-Irish talks in 1940 is the suggestion made some
years later by the British ambassador in Dublin that Lemass
and Ryan had paid a courtesy call to Buckingham Palace;
however, there is no evidence for this unlikely story.[13]

This was not the end of Lemass's dealings with Britain on
supplies. Despite assurances given at the time that Irish-
registered oil tankers (commissioned as part of the refinery
project) had been transferred to the British register, oil ship-
ments to Ireland were seriously restricted. Irish claims to these
tankers were dismissed and Lemass saw this, in a typically
blunt phrase, as a 'double-cross'. He also experienced the
willingness of British commercial interests to use the war-time
situation to secure their own ends. Both oil companies and tea
merchants in London applied these pressures; although
successful in the short term, their longer-term effect was to
strengthen Lemass's old Sinn Féin convictions that Ireland
should aspire to economic as well as political self-determination.

But, for the moment, there was plenty to occupy even his
voracious appetite for work. The possible threat of imminent
invasion in July 1940 led to a government decision to provide
for an alternative structure of regional and county com-
missioners to function in place of the central governmental
administration. The Minister for Supplies was made responsible
for the preparation of necessary plans and within ten days had
presented them to his cabinet colleagues.[14] The episode was
indicative both of the status and efficiency of Lemass.

Other issues proved less tractable. Noticeably, the long
struggle to secure governmental approval for the introduction
of children's allowances shows how powerful colleagues could

delay decision, not only under pressure from Lemass but even from de Valera.[15] The issue was first raised at a government meeting of 11 July 1939 and was obviously contentious. The continuing decline of the population, especially in rural areas, was generally regarded as a criticism of the Irish experiment in national independence; the Commission on Emigration reflected this view in its comment, 'in our view a strongly increasing population should occupy a high place among the criteria by which the success of a national economic policy should be judged.'[16] De Valera himself was known to be interested in the population question and had enshrined the ideal of a maximised rural population in the Constitution. Naturally, then, the earliest proposals from Frank Aiken were concerned to provide family allowances for agricultural workers and small farmers. The immediate reaction was a series of commonly held objections contained in a long memorandum from MacEntee. Some were practical: that the scheme, in essence, was a redistributive proposal which would be expensive to administer and would not achieve its stated objective — 'in order to drive the unfit into matrimony we are to drive the strongest, the most enterprising, the best educated of our young earners out of the country.' Others were theoretical: that Ireland, more than any other predominantly Catholic country, had already carried political equalitarianism to unnatural lengths ('the married man and his wife carrying the whole burden of their families have no more voice in the direction of public affairs than the flapper or whipper-snapper of twenty-one'); that the scheme could further weaken parental authority; that it represented a subtle but significant advance in principle on existing state intervention in social services which could lead to 'the servile state'. It was a battery of arguments that seemed designed to appeal to de Valera.

Nevertheless, on 14 November 1939, the topic was referred to a cabinet committee that seemed calculated to produce a more positive response. It comprised the proposer of the initial scheme, Aiken, and the two departmental ministers most likely to support a rural-based scheme, Agriculture and Lands. The other two members were Ruttledge (Local Government and Public Health) and Lemass. MacEntee was not included. Over the next few months, despite promptings from the

Taoiseach's department, little progress was made — apparently due to delays within the Department of Local Government. [63] At the beginning of April 1940, while Local Government was still proposing further discussions, Lemass attempted to force a decision. He wrote to the secretary to the government:

> I am sending you herewith a document containing an outline of proposals for the payment of allowances to children which it is desired to have submitted to the government. I am asking you to arrange for its circulation as otherwise it is not clear whose responsibility it is. The document has been prepared by me. It has of course no relation to the functions of the Department of Supplies. It has been prepared as a result of the discussion at the cabinet committee on family allowances, of which the Minister for Local Government is chairman. It is in a sense the report of that committee. At the same time it should be clear that it has not been prepared by the committee but that they are recommending its consideration by the government and particularly the proposal in the final paragraph (that, subject to government agreement in principle, an inter-departmental committee of Finance, Local Government and Industry and Commerce prepare the heads of legislation). I will be glad if you will arrange to have it circulated at an early date.

This was too audacious and de Valera was of 'opinion that it would be undesirable to bring proposals' to the government until the views of relevant departments, including Finance and Industry and Commerce, were known. Over the next two-and-a-half years it required repeated pressure from the Taoiseach's Department before a scheme was finally submitted. In the meantime further arguments were advanced about the undesirability of extending the range of direct state intervention. The family allowance issue illustrates not only a typical example of Lemass's impatience with bureaucratic delay but also the very real opposition he was to face as, increasingly, he pondered the problems of devising suitable policies for post-war Ireland. Political inertia, administrative caution, religious conservatism and personal suspicion would all have to be overcome; the road from protection to free trade would be a rocky one.

2

During this period Lemass was more widely involved in public policy than has often been realised. When Michael Mills asked about pressures on Irish neutrality he pleaded lack of knowledge: 'I was not so much involved in this except as a member of the government. I wouldn't have known all the details of what was going on.' In fact, throughout the war he was a member of what amounted to an inner cabinet. This began in May 1940 as the cabinet committee on emergency problems; chaired by de Valera, the core members were Lemass, Aiken (Minister for the Co-ordination of Defensive Measures) and Seán T. O'Kelly (who joined in August 1940).[17] This discussed a wide variety of security issues including plans for intelligence, defence, evacuation and emergency procedures. De Valera chaired all but one of the seventy-four meetings; Lemass was present at all but one. He obviously, then, played a central role between 1940 and 1942 in determining general policy. Given his own interests, perhaps inevitably, the record indicates a continuing concern with economic matters: he suggested contracting the Northern Ireland government regarding electricity supply and supplied information on compulsory tillage for de Valera's Christmas message to the United States in 1940.

Perhaps arising from this, the committee agreed on 2 January 1941 that 'the Minister for Supplies should undertake the organisation of a campaign for increasing food supplies with particular reference to wheat.' This prompted Dr Ryan, the Minister for Agriculture, to complain to de Valera about overlapping of ministerial responsibilities.[18] It seems likely that others also complained. Arising from an Industry and Commerce memorandum in February the government decided that 'matters relating to emergency production should be dealt with by a cabinet committee.' Both MacEntee and Ryan were made members; significantly the chairman was Seán Lemass. Known as 'the economic committee of the cabinet', the membership was expanded to include both Taoiseach and Tánaiste but it only met on four occasions. It ceased to function on 7 April 1941 and business was referred either to the government or the emergency problems committee.

The episode probably represented an effort by other ministers and departments to define and restrict the growing influence of Supplies. It clearly failed. On the contrary, the routine administration of rationing schemes was no longer sufficiently challenging for Lemass. Mrs Lemass reports an often-repeated version of what happened:

> his appetite for work was insatiable and he went and told de Valera that he was bored because there wasn't enough for him to do. De Valera fixed that. He appointed him Minister for Industry and Commerce as well as Minister for Supplies.[19]

It was scarcely that simple. He may well have decided that it was time for him to resume command in his old department. Besides, by now, Lemass was increasingly conscious that he needed to be able to control domestic production as well as distribution and imports in order to secure adequate supplies. Whatever about motivations, when, in August 1941, Ruttledge retired from Local Government due to ill-health he was replaced by Seán MacEntee and Lemass resumed his old Industry and Commerce portfolio in addition to Supplies.

The significance of this development is hinted at in the comment of an astute and well-placed observer:

> With the insight into the industrial situation afforded by his experience as Minister for Supplies, it was natural that Seán Lemass, on his return to Industry and Commerce, should reassess the merits of the policy of hurried and indiscriminate protection pursued in the pre-war years. He was too intelligent a man not to learn from experience and too patriotic to neglect any lessons relevant to the long-term development of the Irish economy.

At the time this reaction was less evident. The supply situation made the policy of protectionism redundant and, in effect, all protective duties were suspended. But public statements gave little clue that while the 'frenetic activity on the day-to-day work was going on to ensure that essential supplies and services were maintained, serious long-term planning for the post-war period' was already in train.[20]

Indeed, the received wisdom of economists and historians still
[66] tends to place the renaissance in government economic thinking and the acceptance of planning in the 1950s.

The real beginning point — typically identifying a problem
with both social and economic implications — is possibly a
memorandum from Lemass to de Valera in June 1942 proposing the establishment of a new Department of Labour to
tackle unemployment, especially with a view to the post-war
prospects.[21] On 30 June an item on the government agenda
was headed 'Planning for post-war situation'. This gave rise to
a discussion on 'the need for systematic planning not merely
to meet pressing problems of the moment but also to provide
for the situation . . . when the emergency comes to an end'
and a decision that:

> the several departments should catalogue and examine
> forthwith the major projects of national development to
> which they had been giving consideration when the Euro-
> pean War broke out and those they have had under con-
> sideration since, take stock of the progress made and push
> consideration to the point where definite proposals could
> be submitted for government approval, final plans detailed
> and all possible preparations made for their immediate
> execution by the respective departments the moment the
> emergency had ended.

This decision with its emphasis on clear decision, specific
action and immediate urgency bears the authentic stamp of
Seán Lemass. To have such a broad decision recorded was,
as Dr Fanning has noted, unique:

> nowhere else in the minutes kept since 1937, nor indeed
> in the minutes for 1922-37, is any similar declaration of
> intent as to the economic policy of the government of the
> day recorded, nor does one find policy statements of a
> comparable kind in the cabinet minutes.[22]

While Dr Fanning's judgment here is accurate, his subsequent
suggestion that this scheme failed to generate the debate on
post-war economic planning is incorrect.

A government decision of 24 November 1942 established
the cabinet committee on economic planning which, in effect,

became the direct descendant of the earlier committees.[23] The new inner cabinet was again chaired by de Valera and was limited to two regular members: the Tánaiste and Minister for Finance, Seán T. O'Kelly, and Lemass. Very occasionally some other minister attended a single meeting, but these three continued to meet weekly over the next two and a quarter years to frame the nation's future. Lemass provided the driving force.

The committee met for the first time on 2 December 1942 and briefly reviewed the departmental replies to the Taoiseach's letter on the subject of post-war development following the June decision. Although a note in the minutes stressed confidentiality, it was scarcely coincidental that on 3 December the Parliamentary Secretary in Finance, Hugo Flinn, wrote a personal letter to the Taoiseach drawing attention to the likely political effects in Ireland of the publication of the Beveridge Plan: it could be 'a "god-send" for the Labour Party and, properly worked, worth quite a few seats' and should be examined at once by the departments directly concerned. In fact the publicity associated with Beveridge and British moves towards a welfare state provided the background to a growing public awareness of the need to consider post-war social and economic change. Two Fine Gael deputies tabled a Dáil motion on 3 February 1943:

> That this House is of opinion that the proposals outlined in the Beveridge Report for the attaining of social security in Britain merit the earnest consideration of the government, and requests that a White Paper be prepared showing the estimated cost of the application of such proposals to this country.[24]

Beveridge also triggered a much less publicised but protracted debate between Irish ministers on the approach to post-war planning. The two main protagonists were MacEntee and Lemass. The former had already directed the attention of colleagues to 'the very marked differences of opinion which exist among Catholic social workers who have studied the question of sociological merits and demerits of family allowances.'[25] He extended the campaign in 1943 with a memorandum on 'Children's Allowances, "Beveridgism" and the Catholic Church', extracted from a letter to the Bishop of [68] Sheffield by a conservative British academic opposing the growth of state intervention, and pointing out conflicts between 'Beveridgism' and Catholic social teaching. Lemass was little concerned with such abstract considerations.

He had already reported to the committee on economic planning that 'arrangements would be made in his Department for an examination of the Beveridge Report as soon as time could be spared from work on preparation of a Children's Allowance Bill.' Meanwhile, his own correspondence with de Valera of 1 December 1942 effectively provided the starting point for the committee's work; this included an extensive series of proposals covering the ESB, civil aviation, ports and harbours, transport, tourism, mineral development and general industrial development. It may not have been a 'national plan' in the sense in which that term would be used later. It certainly implied both a more interventionist role for the state and the need to move beyond protectionism in order to provide economic development. The fact that de Valera presided over the committee as these proposals were developed suggests that his often-quoted St Patrick's Day radio broadcast of 1943, painting an extremely traditional and rural image of 'The Ireland We Have Dreamed Of', may need reinterpretation. For clearly, behind the seemingly immutable commitment to ideals spelled out in the mid-1920s, Fianna Fáil was being pushed into a range of new policies and options.[26]

Lemass, in his own style, was also ambivalent. Introducing the Industry and Commerce estimate for 1943 he spoke of the department's function of industrial stimulation as being 'in abeyance'. Replying to the debate he invited deputies who had raised the question to 'appreciate the difficulty of prescribing a policy for the post-war period in any detail for the present. The post-war conditions, in relation to which that policy will have to be prepared, cannot at present be visualised.' He went further and asked deputies to note that tariffs and other restrictions on imports had been 'suspended' by emergency powers orders of limited duration. He recommended an early post-war resumption of the industrialisation drive.[27] That could scarcely be taken as a retreat from pre-war protectionism. But an election year was not the time to disturb

possible support among the commercial and industrial community.

The Taoiseach hinted at some change in a little-noted
remark concluding the debate on the nomination of ministers
following the 1943 general election when he mentioned that
there was

> at the present time in existence a sub-committee of the
> cabinet that meets every week before ordinary office work
> begins trying to look ahead and to provide as far as we can
> useful employment for those who are likely to return after
> the war. It is trying to develop various schemes so that we
> will be able to get about them with all possible speed the
> moment conditions become normal and when the various
> essential supplies are available.[28]

Those developments extended beyond simple schemes for
continuing protection. In the course of 1943, for instance,
the committee 'decided to ask the Minister for Agriculture
that the committee on agriculture should take note of the
desirability of joining agricultural policy and land purchase',
held two meetings with the Minister for Education, agreed to
proceed with the establishment of a mercantile marine, noted
Industry and Commerce memoranda on port and harbour
and mineral development, and considered giving information
on post-war planning to the Archbishop of Dublin 'in his
capacity as Chairman of the Commission on Youth Unemployment'.

But there were many other more pressing items on the
government agenda as Ireland faced into 1944. The general
supply situation continued to be critical and Leydon paid
three visits to London to improve the position. Despite official
advice from Britain, the United States increased its pressure
on Ireland and Irish troops were put on stand-by in border
areas. Politically, Fianna Fáil's position as a minority government was somewhat eased by internal divisions within the
Labour Party, which led to a split.

Lemass was fully occupied. Apart from the problems
created by the supply situation, he was busy with legislation.
As soon as he had piloted the Children's Allowances Bill
through Dáil and Seanad he was immediately involved in a new

bill to amend the Conditions of Employment Act 1936.[29] He
[70] was working to improve industrial relations and also, despite
much publicised allegations of stock manipulation, he pressed
ahead with a major Transport Bill. The episode marks two pro-
nounced aspects of Lemass's career as the war drew to an end:
a whisper campaign of rumours, and a progressive shift from
the pre-war emphasis on creating Irish industry to the post-war
emphasis on the need for competitive efficiency.

The rumours (some at least in part encouraged from within
his own party) ranged from inflated stories about his card-
playing habits to allegations of corruption. They touched
Lemass in a sensitive spot and were to persist. He took a strict
view of personal integrity; family and close civil servants have
commented on his insistent propriety in refusing gifts and
favours. He compared his position with that of a fellow-victim,
the chairman of the Great Southern Railways company:

> He has never been a politician and, therefore has never been
> the victim of a smear campaign, as the Americans call it.
> Those of us who have had that experience are not so much
> inclined to be perturbed, because we know that from our
> experience that when the truth comes out it rebounds,
> and rebounds with boomerang effect, on those who started
> the campaign.[30]

But despite the public stance, he found the rumours hurtful
and made the point to the present author that when leaving
office in 1948 he did not take a paper with him; a challenge
to opponents to substantiate these allegations. In fact neither
then nor later was there anything in his life-style or possessions
to give any credible support to the round of rumours and
innuendos.

Lemass's long introductory speech on the Transport Bill
gave some further public indication of his broader thinking on
post-war development:[31]

> The government contemplates that the immediate post-war
> situation will be one of critical significance in the future
> economic development of the country. It is our view that
> we should get ourselves organised now in every important
> economic sphere to face the problems and to avail of the

opportunities which the post-war period may bring. It is contemplated that other measures to that end will also [71] be introduced. . . . Our national economic development requires that our public services, including our transport services, should be thoroughly efficient. It requires also that they should be self-supporting. . . . Whatever theoretical case may be made for competition in encouraging efficiency or stimulating enterprise in other commercial spheres, it can, in relation to transport, undermine the stability of the services which are necessary to the national commercial life and it can, in its effect, do irreparable damage to the public interest. . . . Our national economic efficiency, our competitive effectiveness in international trade, depend not merely upon the actual charges for public transport in operation but upon the total of the overhead burden that industry and agriculture must carry. . . . Under a national-ised system of transport, coupled with a democratic govern-ment, the direction of transport services would be under-taken, not for the purpose of promoting national economic development, but for the purpose of forwarding party political causes. . . . We have in recent years extended state ownership or state regulation in the economic field to a considerable extent . . . we have experiemented with different types of organisation . . . the aim of the govern-ment in devising methods of controlling these various concerns was, first of all, to ensure that the government should have control in matters of general policy and, secondly, to see that these concerns should have complete freedom in matters of day-to-day management, but particularly to see that such concerns would be free from anything in the way of political pressure. . . . The govern-ment has never been satisifed that it has yet devised a satisfactory organisation or method for the carrying out of that type of enterprise.

Here, in a single speech, are the main elements in Lemass's thinking in the mid-forties and later: an emphasis on efficiency, international competitiveness, experimentation and the commitment to the mixed economy. This was a pragmatic approach that rejected ideology.

It provides perhaps a clue to Lemass's uncharacteristically [72] intemperate reaction to the *Report of the Commission on Vocational Organisation*. Published after Fianna Fáil had secured a new majority in a snap election, the report not merely reproduced the complaints of the Federation of Irish Manufacturers about the lack of consultation and information by the Department of Industry and Commerce but concluded that

> the record of representations made to the Minister by the Federation of Irish Manufacturers in 1938-39 shows that events have amply justified their recommendations, and that the Minister in refusing to accept them committed a serious mistake.[32]

This was too much for Lemass. As a professional administrator he was committed to the idea of consultation with interests; as a politician he believed in the concept of ministerial responsibility; as an experienced negotiator he knew how easily amateurs could underestimate the implications of policy. The Department of Supplies 'Record of Activities', in a section on 'Relations with Trade Organisations' provides a summary of Lemass's views:

> It was always made clear to associations and to industrialists generally that consultation was for the purpose of securing advice derived from practical experience; all decisions rested with the Minister who took full responsibility for what the Department did or omitted to do. It was necessary to insist on this position. After the outbreak of war the Federation of Irish Manufacturers proposed that its organisation should discharge some of the Department's functions. This offer was declined. It was found too that in private negotiations in Britain and in other matters one or two of the more prominent industrialists were disposed to enter into commitments which could have a definite bearing on the country's future trade without first consulting the Department.

Already subjected to both personal and political criticism he was not prepared to accept what he described as 'the querulous, nagging, propagandist tone of . . . such a slovenly document'.

The acrimonious note in Lemass's subsequent newspaper controversy with the Bishop of Galway may have owed something to his resistance to clerical encroachments in the political sphere. It also reflected the frustrations of an active minister being reined in by more cautious colleagues.

After a break in its work over the period of the 1944 election the cabinet committee on economic planning had resumed activity. It was decided to give early attention to post-war agricultural aims and activities. There was more of Lemass than de Valera in the committee's minute:

> with regard to other economic and developmental activities which had already from time to time been the subject of detailed consideration by the committee, it was decided that, in future, the committee should aim at avoiding the consideration of matters of detail and should endeavour to concentrate on broadly reviewing the progress of departments in the advancement of their plans, in the preparation of necessary legislation and generally in bringing their preparatory measures to the most advanced stage practicable in existing circumstances.[33]

In fact the committee became the forum for an important discussion illustrating significant differences within the Fianna Fáil government on agricultural policy.

Joined by Ryan for a preliminary discussion on the topic, the committee initially stressed three central aims: the need to increase agricultural production, the importance of the export market, and 'the importance, from the national and social point of view, of the maintenance on the land in economic security of as many families as might be practicable'. That remained the public stance: a reflection of the views enunciated in the Constitution and repeated by de Valera in the much quoted St Patrick's Day broadcast of the previous year. But an unusually detailed note of a subsequent meeting shows Lemass challenging his leader's policy. The note records that the Taoiseach had expressed his view that the government's land policy aimed both to maximise the number of farm families and to secure the efficient production of the nation's food. Seán Lemass spoke next and felt it was desirable to determine clearly what was the primary aim of the policy. If land policy is to be an instrument of agricultural output to be used with a view to putting agricultural policy on an efficient basis, then it should be directed accordingly. He thought himself that the success of any plan for the placing of agricultural industry on an efficient basis must depend to a considerable extent on land policy. The policy could, of course, take into account the desirability of placing as many people on the land as possible. He agreed there was a special problem of congestion and that this must be dealt with. Consideration could be given to the possibility of devoting all available land to the relief of congestion. He also strongly advocated the publication of a White Paper stating clearly the government's land policy with a view to ending any uncertainty which might prevail.

While the later remarks might appear to have softened the impact of Lemass's central emphasis on efficiency, this was still a challenge. It was clear that by now the government could not devote 'all available land' to the relief of congestion. Whatever about de Valera's stated belief 'that there was more real work and thrift on small farms', Lemass was pushing towards larger and more efficient farms; he was increasingly emphasising the need to expand industry in order to provide employment.

Immediately after the election, speaking on his departmental estimate he argued that in the second phase of Irish post-war recovery,

> the promotion of a high level of employment here will depend, firstly, upon the efficiency of the production methods which we employ; secondly, upon the adequacy and efficiency of our transport and distribution facilities; and, thirdly, upon our capacity to maintain exports in highly competitive markets.[34]

He developed the theme in a wide-ranging speech to the Insurance Institute on 3 December 1944 which stressed that industrial exports meant large-scale industries, that success would require adequate finance, the help of government and

trade unions and the good-will of the community, and then
ended:

we have the men who will make the effort, provided it
is understood that they are working in conformity with
agreed national policy, and that no swing of the political
pendulum will result in an abrupt reversal of plans.[35]

Privately, too, he was urging his senior colleagues in the
economic planning committee to adopt new, tough, challenging
policies. In January 1945 they agreed with him on the need
for 'an immediate employment policy' but when he attempted
to translate this into a 'full employment policy' they felt the
need to dampen his enthusiasm. In April 1945, after forty-nine
closed meetings, the membership of the committee was
extended to all ministers; by June, meetings were being
cancelled and the committee ceased to exist. In June, when
Seán T. O'Kelly was elected President, Frank Aiken asked for
and was given the vacancy in Finance. It was not an appointment designed to make Lemass's task easier.[36]

Internal governmental inertia seemed to have little effect
on his output and energies. The record of weekly departmental
conferences gives some indication of the variety of topics
demanding Lemass's attention. There might be twenty or more
items on the agenda ranging from small-scale specifics to broad
issues of policy. A typical meeting in August 1945 included
the pricing of razor blades; the manufacture of sulphate of
ammonia; tillage regulations; an application from the Office of
Public Works seeking exemption from lighting and life-saving
regulations (refused); specific applications for special petrol
allowances; a decision to issue a severe warning to seven master
butchers detected using their vans to attend a trade association
meeting; a request to receive a deputation on the Wet Time
Act (approved); the selection of personnel for reappointment
to the Road Transport Advisory Board and for the twenty-
seventh International Labour Conference in Paris.[37] The last
two items raised the increasingly sensitive issue of choosing
trade union representatives.

Lemass had always maintained a good working relationship
with the trade union movement.[38] In measure this reflected
his personal and constituency identification with the Dublin

working man; in measure it represented his ministerial recognition that it made for better administration. During his brief absence from Industry and Commerce, despite union objections, the 1941 Trade Union Act was pushed through the Dáil. Lemass did not speak out at any stage but on his return negotiated a series of changes incorporated in the 1942 amending act which he introduced into the Dáil as an agreed measure. He also softened the rigours of the original wages standstill order. In Charles McCarthy's words he

> managed to combine a warm, co-operative approach to the trade union movement with a steely approach to the Labour Party on the general grounds that his party, Fianna Fáil, was more representative politically of the bulk of trade union members than was the Labour Party, which on a headcount was manifestly true.

He applied policy, as far as possible, both to promote the unity of organised labour and to strengthen the role of Irish-based unions, especially the Irish Transport and General Workers' Union. When the trade union movement split into two Congresses, Lemass maintained relations with both the original ITUC and the newly-formed CIU. His preference, however, was well illustrated in decisions at the Industry and Commerce conference mentioned above. Asked whether both Congresses should be asked to nominate to the Road Transport Advisory Board, the decision was that only the CIU should be invited. On the question of Irish representation at the International Labour Conference, both Congresses had made submissions: 'the Minister took the view that nominees of the CIU should be selected as representatives of work people.' It is probable that only the Supreme Court judgment in the NUR case, upholding the constitutional right to freedom of association, restrained him from a more open attempt to suppress the British-based unions by regulation. Instead he pressed ahead with the Industrial Relations Bill which occupied the greater part of his time in 1946. In essence this created the Labour Court on the basis of a general agreement between unions and employers: 'this was to Lemass only a part of a larger strategy, the first step in this country towards a voluntary, integrated prices and incomes policy, supported by statutory institutions.' In fact, despite the early work of the Labour Court, post-war adjustments triggered a series of major industrial disputes which, significantly, involved teachers and bank officials as well as busmen and industrial workers.

That was only one factor in a growing mood of public discontent that overshadowed other policy initiatives by Lemass in this period. He had pressed ahead with plans for further electricity, turf and aviation development; established Bórd na Móna, Irish Steel, the Shannon Free Airport Development Company, and the Institute for Industrial Research and Standards, as well as representing Ireland at trade talks in London and Paris. He continued to push against the conservatism of the Department of Finance and of colleagues unwilling to share his sense of urgency. On occasions this involved him in public statements that were less than frank about his real intentions. In 1946 he denied that his estimate speech represented 'any change in the policy of the government in relation to industrial development' and said, 'I am in favour of keeping additional powers to interfere with industry at the minimum.'[39] But, despite the controversy over the vocational organisation report, he was taking a tougher line with his old associates in the Federation of Irish Manufacturers, refusing to give them any great preference in regard to information on new industries or consultation on the detail of legislation prior to its submission to the Oireachtas.[40] Although he was still prepared to operate protectionism, it was made clear within Industry and Commerce that

> the aim should be to get away from the policy of restricting manufacture and trade to its pre-war channels and pegging it down to pre-war levels and to facilitate the establishment of new industries as far as possible.

And, publicly, there was a repeated insistence on the theme of competitive efficiency; Lemass told the Dáil in 1947:

> We cannot have everything we want in this world. If we want to make sure of a reasonable and improving standard of living, a widening field of employment and the development of a workable economic system, we must not merely make the effort necessary to step up production but we

must also do so on a basis that will keep the level of prices here in line with prices elsewhere and increase our exportable surplus of goods in a manner that will give a fair prospect of holding our place in competitive international markets.

Lemass revealed how far he was prepared to push government intervention in the economy in his Industrial Efficiency and Prices Bill, introduced on 3 July 1947. This was a judicious mix of carrot and stick, designed both to establish development councils to aid industry and to give the Minister wide-ranging powers to intervene directly.[41] He was also advocating a more active participation by Ireland in European reconstruction and even in a customs union; to a large extent his thinking on this was influenced by his experience in bi-lateral negotiations with Britain and represented a divergence of opinion with de Valera.

But much more mundane political issues were overtaking considerations of high policy throughout these years. The pace and tone of parliamentary politics was increasingly hostile as a frustrated and fragmented opposition united in a common aim: to 'get them out.' The unsettled industrial relations situation, the need to extend rationing, and the inability to control inflation combined to increase pressure on government. So did mounting speculation about corruption in high places. There were three tribunals in succession to investigate allegations about a parliamentary secretary's involvement in a Monaghan bacon factory, about stock exchange manipulation of railway shares, and about the circumstances in which Locke's distillery in Kilbeggan was sold. Seán Lemass was a particular target of the rumour factory created in the two latter cases. It was hinted that he had improperly authorised dubious foreign financiers to purchase the moribund Locke distillery; ironically, the departmental records of the time suggest an almost racist aspect to his ministerial efforts to exclude undesirable aliens.[42] Although the tribunals exonerated Lemass and all other ministers completely, the mood of distrust and discontent was not dissipated. It found expression in two newer political groupings — Clann na Talmhan and Clann na Poblachta. The latter was given the opportunity to challenge the hegemony of Fianna Fáil as it introduced a severe supplementary budget. Whereas Fianna Fáil had won four of the six by-elections in 1945-6, it lost two of three in October 1947 to Clann na Poblachta.

Lemass was in London when the results were declared. According to his own account, de Valera telephoned to ask, 'what would you do?' and he replied 'You are not the man I think you are if the Dáil is not dissolved before I get back.'[43] Subsequently he had doubts about this advice. But he threw himself into the campaign with characteristic vigour and made a marked effort to retain his party's working-class support.

When the results were announced it was clear that Fianna Fáil had lost support, though not as disastrously as Fine Gael. Indeed, like other observers, he expected Fianna Fáil to form a minority government. The *Irish Independent*'s political correspondent anticipated that the National Labour group and about four Independents would vote for de Valera and that three or four others would abstain.[44] Lemass's own recollection to Michael Mills was that

> we did not think we had lost the election. Remember, that the National Labour Party at the time fought the election on the basis that they were going to support a Fianna Fáil government. . . . Up to the night before the Dáil met we did not realise there was going to be a majority against us.

But after sixteen years in government, he was out of office, for a very broad anti-Fianna Fáil coalition was formed and secured a majority under John A. Costello. He could look back over the two decades of parliamentary endeavour to a record of extraordinary achievement. The young gunman turned politician had become the most accomplished ministerial craftsman of his generation. The man who had done so much to create Fianna Fáil was now its deputy leader. He seemed poised, at the height of his considerable powers, to take the next step forward and upward in his political career. But Seán Lemass was to wait another decade before fulfilling his manifest destiny by becoming Taoiseach.

5
The Leader in Waiting

Seán Lemass was not prepared for electoral defeat in 1948.[1]
He had not anticipated that the barely-formed Clann na
Poblachta would do so well and did not envisage the possibility
that National Labour could be coaxed into a governmental
team that included the Labour Party. When the inter-party
government was formed it was clear that politically and
personally a major adjustment to new circumstances was
required. He learned that reality soon enough. On 18 February
1948, as an ex-minister, he was driven home in a state car;
next morning he had to borrow his son's old car ('Noel's
banger') to get into the city. Lemass immediately bought a
modest Ford saloon. Subsequently when invited to become
a director of Lincoln and Nolan, the main Austin agents, it
was embarrassing to drive a rival model but he could not
afford to change cars again. It was an eloquent response to
the spate of rumours about his financial affairs.

In fact he was considerably better off out of office than
he had ever been in his ministerial years. Apart from his
parliamentary earnings, he was immediately appointed to the
board of Irish Press Ltd, and made managing director. This was
no sinecure. Typically he settled down to learn his new trade;
according to a report in the *Irish Times* he went to London to
study newspaper production with the *Daily Mail*.[2] He became
a familiar figure to those already working in the *Press* and
made a major contribution to the launching of Burgh Quay's
most successful paper, the *Sunday Press*. He also joined the
board of Fleming's Fire Clay, Athy, and contributed articles
to the *Irish Press*, while carrying a major parliamentary
responsibility for his party. He found himself amply rewarded
for his range of new duties. To some extent, he was conscious

of the danger of becoming too comfortable with his lot.

Certainly his family recall this as a particularly happy time. [81]
Mrs Lemass noted that he had more time to spend with the
children in the evening and on holidays. They found him more
carefree than ever before. He enjoyed the forgotten freedom
of driving his own car. It was as though this fifty-year-old
public man was trying to make up for lost time and recovering
something of his own youth as he took off with the family
in the car, sometimes singing an old favourite of his soldiering
days, 'Wrap the Green Flag round me, boys'.

He still managed to make an impressive, if secondary,
contribution to Irish political life in these first years back in
opposition. Even before de Valera departed to the United
States, Lemass was effectively the leader of the opposition; he
alone spoke on the nomination of government. Subsequently
he opened for Fianna Fáil both on the vote on account, on the
budget debate, on the referral back of the estimate for the
Department of the Taoiseach as well (as might have been
expected) as on his old Department of Industry and Commerce and on the debate on the Anglo-Irish Trade Agreement.[3]
He was also enmeshed in several controversies about the
purchase of Argentinian wheat (on the grounds that he had
delayed decision, paid too much, and bought directly through
a 'foreign agent' rather than through grain importers), his
alleged use of departmental papers in newspaper articles,
departmental decisions on discontinuing hard-won turf
schemes, and accusations of political patronage in labour
exchange temporary appointments.[4] Some astute and dis-
interested observers were surprised that he allowed so much
to pass uncontradicted. They were not aware of that decision
not to remove papers which would have enabled him to deal
more effectively with many of the charges made. It was one
of the few decisions he regretted; he would not repeat the
mistake in 1954.

This initial period in opposition, 1948-51, was not the most
distinguished phase in Lemass's career. There was little evidence
that his thinking on future economic policy developed. There
is ample evidence of a willingness to play the parliamentary
game of adversary politics. But perhaps the most frequently
quoted example – his original hostility to the establishment

of the Industrial Development Authority and subsequent
[82] enthusiasm to develop it — requires some examination. So,
too, does the divergence between Lemass and de Valera on
the repeal of the External Relations Act. Finally, the question
of an apparent decline in his standing in the party at this time
is worth consideration.

Lemass wasted no time before indulging in what was to
become an extended parliamentary sparring match with his
successor as Minister for Industry and Commerce. Although
Dan Morrissey had been a deputy since 1922, he had no
previous ministerial experience and, like other colleagues in
the inter-party government, had some difficulty adjusting to
his new status. Some intemperate remarks about officials were
reported in the press and taken up by Lemass in the Dáil.[5]
This must have aggravated the difficulties as the Department
of Industry and Commerce adjusted to a new minister after a
decade and a half with Seán Lemass. Relations between
Morrissey and his officials became excessively formal. Some of
them, including Leydon, saw in the original, rather unclear,
proposal to establish an Industrial Development Authority
a reduction of ministerial and departmental control; others,
working within the section affected, interpreted it as an effort
by Morrissey to resolve the problem created by the internal
strains between minister and civil servants.[6]

Against this background, it is easier to understand the
vehemence of Lemass's objection to the new semi-state
organisation. The proposal to establish the IDA was announced
by the Government Information Bureau on 12 February
1949. Quickly Lemass mounted a sustained attack. He
repeatedly used the analogy of the IDA as a fifth wheel and
charged that 'Irish industry is being asked now to show its
merit by winning the race for increased productivity dragging
a cart, a cart without wheels.'[7] There was substance to these
criticisms in terms of the actual operations of the original
IDA, which consisted of former officials of Industry and
Commerce doing the same tasks for the IDA that they had
done for the Department. On the other hand, Lemass's
attempts to condemn the measure as anti-industrial, his
antipathy to at least one member of the Authority and his
switch from opposition to support on resuming government

indicates an undoubtedly partisan colouring to his campaign. At the same time there is no doubt that the functions of the IDA were more precisely defined and executed when Lemass returned to Industry and Commerce. He spelled out the differences shortly after the 1951 general election.[8]

Lemass's apparent switch of policy on the IDA has sometimes been seen as a purely cynical political manoeuvre. The evidence shows that it was more than this. Even his interventions on the committee stage of the IDA Bill indicate a less negative purpose than has sometimes been suggested. There is the further point that a political opponent and former parliamentary secretary in Industry and Commerce, Liam Cosgrave, agreed with Lemass that it was a mistake to have the IDA 'in the position in which it was, neither in nor out of a government department.'[9] But it is also clear that there were mixed motives for some changes in Lemass's views; he would, as he told one of his civil servants, have been a fool not to use a device like the Prices Advisory Body, which he attacked when it was established by his predecessor, to protect himself from the odium of unpopular decisions.

Publicly Lemass's response to the proposal to repeal the External Relations Act was a long, historical and partisan speech.[10] Privately, according to his own account, he had already been urging de Valera to take this further step; he thought that during the war years Irish neutrality could have been compromised by the ambiguity of the Act; de Valera had seen the connection with the British crown as a possible tool to end partition. Moreover, despite the partisan tone of his speeches on the subject, Lemass made no bones about welcoming the step – he even expressed some regret that it had not been done by a Fianna Fáil government. This public expression of opinion caused some dissent within the party and added to criticism of Lemass.

It was another indication of the carry-over in this opposition period of tensions, based on personality as well as policy differences, between senior men in the party. Lemass told Michael Mills:

As far as Fianna Fáil was concerned, there was a risk which we fully recognised that the great organisation which we had built up throughout the country would begin to disintegrate when it found the party for the first time in opposition. So we embarked on a very vigorous re-organisation campaign in which the members of the previous government were free to participate; so that by 1951 we had a much more effective organisation than we had in 1948.

Privately he was more critical of his colleagues. Although the files of the *Irish Press* in this period reveal former ministers addressing party meetings and report the establishment of new cumainn, there was no serious re-organisation.[11] There had been no serious analysis of the 1948 election and the general view in the parliamentary party seemed to be that opposition was a temporary interlude in the long reign of Fianna Fáil in government, that the inter-party group would break down of its own accord and that there was no need for Fianna Fáil to commit itself to any definite policy or programme. Lemass found the shadow cabinet which met in this period unhelpful; no firm lines of responsibility were drawn and all were encouraged to intervene on all topics. He himself carried a considerable part of the burden of parliamentary opposition. De Valera, in his view, showed a rather inert attitude and tended to become the judge of other people's ideas rather than the initiator of policy and the driving force in solving political problems. At the same time the Chief did intervene to head off a motion at the party's ard fheis for yet another public enquiry on allegations of corruption. But there were no study groups to continue the early post-war planning enterprise. Perhaps it was just as well since the party returned to power as a minority government in 1951.

Indeed the indications are that Lemass was reluctant enough to accept office. He told Michael Mills:

I did not welcome the prospect of coming back into government in the conditions of 1951 at all. If we had won a majority on our own in that election it would have been different. Indeed, during that period after the 1951 election when it was not certain how the Independents were going to vote I made no personal effort to influence any of them as to how they were going to vote because I realised that whoever got their support and became the government was going to have a difficult time. It was not our most successful period in office, as you know. [85]

A number of factors coincided to create a trough in his career. Against Lemass's wishes, de Valera put MacEntee back into Finance; it was a deliberately conservative choice.[12] There was little renewal of government; only one senior minister, P. J. Little, was let go and only two new men appointed. Lemass was also much more conscious than formerly that de Valera's own political powers were failing. Moreover, he himself was feeling the strain and would soon be forced to take time off to undergo a gall-bladder operation.

Little of this showed on the surface. The transition back into office was smooth enough. Neither his family nor civil servants noted any change in his attitude or work pattern. The government was appointed on 14 June 1951; the weekly departmental conference resumed on 18 June and a month later on the estimate for Industry and Commerce, Lemass spelled out his policy.[13] This included retention of both the IDA and the Prices Advisory Body, an insistence that the ESB follow his preferred option that 'all future electrical development will be based on turf and water power' rather than on imported fuels, and a holding statement in regard to the Great Northern Railway Company, and the Irish shipping and air companies. Although some handsome tributes had been paid to Lemass in the debate on the nomination of government, this initial contribution suggests that he had returned to his old department with few new ideas.[14] It was to be business as usual. But there was no obvious new policy departure, no impetus to push forward. Perhaps because of his health problems at this stage in his career, Lemass was uncharacteristically lacking in departmental or governmental initiatives.

The overall economic climate was not encouraging for policy innovation.[15] There could be no serious doubt about his own preferred choice. But realistically he accepted that in all the circumstances action had to be delayed. Lemass went along with the government's two severe budgets of 1951 and 1952; accompanying MacEntee at Anglo-Irish talks in London on the sterling crisis in February 1952, he accepted the need 'to co-operate in measures designed to strengthen sterling convertibility'. In later years he looked back critically to the conservatism of the Fianna Fáil government in the period 1951-4; the contemporary records suggest that, like the rest of his colleagues, he saw financial stability as a more urgent priority than economic development.

It is also likely that at this stage health was a factor limiting the performance of ministers. Lemass's own gall-bladder trouble eventually required an operation. During his convalescence — perhaps in an effort to occupy and extend recuperation — de Valera recommended him to resume his study of Irish and offered some books. Lemass was no linguist. His attitude to Irish mirrored that of most of his compatriots: a ready willingness to praise and recommend the revival of the language, the occasional use of standard phrases, but a reluctance to make any serious personal effort to learn or commit himself to learn the language. The family recall their father, pencil in hand, beside the wireless, intent on the 'Listen and Learn' programme. But there was always something else to do and the effort did not last. He was similarly resistant to de Valera's encouragement and was soon asking visitors to send him something to read on economics. Soon he was back at the office looking for something to do.

If there was little movement on the major development fronts, Lemass was not idle. His continued interest in tourism was reflected in the creation of An Tóstal, a tourist festival that never achieved the goals he intended. He soon reversed some of the adverse decisions taken by the inter-party government affecting favoured projects inaugurated in his earlier ministerial career: the transatlantic air service was revived; Irish Steel was encouraged to expand the range and output of their industry; the ESB was pushed into further turf-burning generation stations; and Lemass's original plan for an overseas marketing board emerged in modified form as Córas Tráchtála.

He busied himself with legislation, although this tended to be less radical than he might have wished. The need to encourage a wider dispersal of industrial development was reflected in the Underdeveloped Areas Bill, another inching forward of Lemass's plans to modernise rural Ireland. The opposition argued that the bill was a partisan effort to boost Fianna Fáil's declining support in western areas. Lemass responded with a typically realistic political calculation: there was no guarantee of success and besides 'the weakest foundation on which to build political prospects is gratitude.'[16]

He was again ready to push legislative proposals to establish 'a competent and independent authority' to monitor trade union activity. A somewhat similar problem had been developing on the other side of the industrial divide. Three decades of protection had encouraged the growth of a multiplicity of unco-ordinated trade associations which frequently worked to limit competition in the interests of their own members. Lemass was not prepared to trust voluntary arrangements to correct the situation. He introduced the Restrictive Trade Practices Bill.[17] It was a broad based measure influenced in part by the British Monopolies and Restrictive Practices Act as well as by American and New Zealand legislation studied by Lemass. It provoked considerable opposition. The Associated Chambers of Commerce in a circular to deputies claimed that Irish circumstances did not justify such 'drastic' action. Trade associations which Lemass himself had encouraged as Minister for Supplies urged rejection. Although individual Fine Gael speakers raised a variety of differing criticism — in particular legal deputies urged a more careful definition of terms — there was no division on the second reading. Nevertheless, his political opponents, and noticeably Patrick McGilligan, underscored the extent to which the bill represented a withdrawal by Lemass from the far more radical provisions of his Industrial Prices and Efficiency Bill.

That was a fair point. Replying to the estimate debate for the Department of Industry and Commerce in October 1953 he was challenged about reviving the Prices and Efficiency Bill. Although professing 'a very deep affection for that Bill', he refused to commit himself to its reintroduction.[18] It was a further indication of Lemass's unresolved ambiguity on the issue of state intervention and coercion. He remained committed to the idea of a mixed economy and ready to distinguish between the proper functions of private and public enterprise. And there was little hint of radicalism in his remark about the need to reform Irish banking:

> I think it is true that the financial institutions of this state were not specifically designed to foster the economic development of a free Ireland. . . . I am convinced also that their reform must come gradually and, if possible, voluntarily.[19]

Allowing for these reservations and in the face of the indifference and antipathy of more conservative colleagues, Lemass continued to think about and plan for future policy direction. It is evident that he was increasingly disenchanted by his own pre-war protectionist policies in the circumstances of the post-war world. There was the danger that lack of competition could encourage manufacturers to palm off inferior goods; perhaps, he thought, the Institute for Industrial Research and Standards could be used to originate standard specification orders.[20] Throughout 1953 he was involved in an internal government debate as he tried to prod his colleagues out of the inertia induced by a mood of conservative uncertainty.[21]

In January he submitted a memorandum advocating initial tax free allowances for capital equipment and the liberalisation of depreciation provisions. Finance, of course, opposed. He returned to the attack in a memorandum of 28 July, in response to a rather general public statement by de Valera on the unemployment problem. Lemass argued that 'there appears to be no practical alternative to an enlarged programme of state investment'. Initially submitted to the cabinet committee on the provision of employment, his plan for 25,000 new jobs drew a sharp response from Finance:

> It may be questioned whether the Minister for Industry and Commerce believes that our economy is viable. A negative view is indeed possible, especially in the present divided state of the national territory.

But the red herring of partition did not block the eventual creation of the National Development Fund in 1954. Lemass also won a partial victory for his capital taxation proposals by the creation of a Commission of Inquiry into Taxation in October 1953.

These back-room battles had little effect on the surface of Irish politics and no immediate effects on the problems publicly confronting Lemass: rising prices, industrial unrest and an insecure parliamentary position. For the first time the unemployed began to organise; marches through the streets began in Lemass's own constituency and led to confrontations with the Gardaí directly outside the Dáil, as well as protest sit-downs on O'Connell Bridge. Although, with the help of a group of independent deputies, the government carried a confidence motion in July 1953 Lemass was under no illusions about Fianna Fáil's prospects. Concluding the debate he admitted:

> The outstanding problem still is unemployment, ... We accept that the work we have done has not been wide enough in its scope or pushed ahead as vigorously as it should have been.[22]

Lemass's analysis of Fianna Fáil's failure did not stop with general principles and pious parliamentary platitudes. He remained an organisation man, well aware that the party he had done so much to develop more than a quarter of a century earlier was in need of overhaul. On 23 November 1953 the national executive of Fianna Fáil accepted the recommendations of its officer board and established a department of organisation under a director who was, subject to the authority of the honorary secretaries, 'given full executive powers in matters concerning organisation, publicity, and propaganda including power to control the activities of all officers engaged in these branches of work.'[23] A clue to Lemass's influence on this decision was the further decision to offer an appointment as organiser in headquarters to Joe O'Neill, his own constituency organiser in Dublin South-Central. A week later Matt Feehan was appointed director of organisation but there was scarcely time to begin work before an election was called. On 8 March 1954, Lemass was appointed national director of elections and following the party's defeat on 12 July 1954 he took over as director of organisation.

Apart from the burden of his parliamentary duties, this was to be Lemass's full-time job in the period 1954-7. He was determined to restore the party's sagging electoral fortunes. That decline had been mirrored in his own electoral performance. In the new five-seat Dublin South-Central constituency in 1948 he had captured over 13,000 first-preference votes.

By 1951 this dipped to 10,759, although the Fianna Fáil share rose from 43.5 per cent to 55.1 per cent. In 1954 Lemass (still heading the poll) had dropped to a personal vote of 7,753 and the party share declined to 41.4 per cent.

Lemass was empowered to nominate an organisation committee and recruited, among others, Kevin Boland, C. J. Haughey and Eoin Ryan. He added other young men, including Brian Lenihan, to this ginger-group. They provided not only a task force for the immediate work of reorganisation but also the backbone of ministerial and party leadership in the next two decades. By early September he had planned a series of reorganising meetings throughout the country, explained to his young lieutenants the purpose of the exercise, and invited their suggestions. In fact a great deal of the initial national survey of the Fianna Fáil machine was carried out by Lemass himself.

Once again, as in the 1920s, he travelled around the country. Originally he had used his old Volunteer contacts to seek out men in different localities around whom the new organisation could be built. Now he was probing that organisation, judging its local strengths and weaknesses, preparing where necessary to encourage the substitution of new candidates for the old men he himself had recruited. Companions recall the long journeys through rural Ireland: he could drive for a hundred miles without exchanging a word of conversation, concentrating perhaps on the mission at the end of the journey. He was not a man to waste either speech or time. Commonly he carried a bar of chocolate in his pocket, rather than be delayed *en route* stopping for snacks and being buttonholed in casual encounters. Still it was a less intense Lemass than the young man of the twenties; by the mid-fifties, if the opportunity arose, he was ready to plan his journey to take in a couple of early races at the Curragh before carrying on.

Yet he did not lose sight of the central objective. He would carefully check the reports of his team and swiftly act on them. For the first time a serious effort was made to draw up proper membership lists. The 'paper' or 'ghost' cumainn, so often used by local candidates to secure renomination or to exclude rivals, were rigorously investigated. Note was made of organisational gaps and the local party encouraged to establish new cumainn or break up over-large ones, and to cater for areas of neglect. Similarly he prepared the ground for a generational shift in leadership throughout the party. Such an organisational renaissance could only be accomplished by a particular combination of experience, information, will and authority. It confirmed in a practical way at all levels of Fianna Fáil the promised succession of Lemass announced by de Valera.

Looking back on these years, the younger men recall the reorganisation enterprise in terms of excitement, exhilaration and achievement. Lemass seemed fully to share that positive mood. He was always ready to listen to and consider their suggestions. He forged powerful bonds of shared experience with a group a generation removed from his own. If he had any regrets as he revitalised the party at the expense of the old-timers, he typically masked that emotion behind his cultivated façade of disciplined detachment. Perhaps he felt no pangs. Certainly in later years he was clearly of the opinion, though in a slightly different context, that 'there are too many people who have stayed on too long' and was prone to say that not enough young blood had been brought into Fianna Fáil in this intensive three-year organisation campaign.[24]

Lemass also understood that Fianna Fáil needed renewing at the level of policy. Simultaneously with his overhaul of the party machinery he set himself to shape a new set of priorities for the party. Crudely these could be represented as substituting a set of defined social and economic objectives for the rather diffuse constitutional and nationalist aims articulated by de Valera. Such an interpretation does less than justice to both men. For Lemass never lost his commitment to the central goals of Irish nationalism and de Valera had never been indifferent to the practical problems of social and economic development. However, in the mid-fifties Lemass saw more clearly than his Chief the need to articulate and order the priorities of a party offering itself for government to an Ireland heading into the 1960s.

New structures within the Fianna Fáil organisation served a double purpose: they provided a new source for wider recruitment outside the traditional ranks of the party and were an excellent platform from which to stimulate a debate about policy. Both Cómh-Chomhairle Átha Clíath and Cáirde Fáil were developed with this dual aim. The constitution of Cómh-Chomhairle identified it as a 'unit of Fianna Fáil' but allowed that associated membership might be given to 'any person whether resident in Ireland or not and whether a member of the Fianna Fáil organisation or not'. Its stated purpose committed Cómh-Chomhairle in particular to the task of initiating public discussions of the aims of Fianna Fáil. It became a prod by which Lemass could nudge colleagues in the shadow cabinet and parliamentary party into new and more specific policy commitments. Cómh-Chomhairle organised lectures and discussions and deliberately provoked debate, especially on economic issues, designed to force Fianna Fáil to a new programme in government. A perceptive contemporary profile noted:

> Lemass has already shown distinctive signs of imaginative courage and resilience which goes to make a really great minister; and he has succeeded in shaking off some of the shackles of the past. . . . Lemass's warnings on the hitherto neglected front of tariff-protected industry are now taken seriously by those most immediately affected.[25]

Just how seriously and radically his economic thinking had developed was revealed in a much publicised address to Comh-Chomhairle Átha Clíath in Clery's Ballroom on 11 October 1955. This quickly became part of the Lemass legend. Political opponents accused him of a crude attempt to bribe the electorate with the promise of 100,000 jobs and for the next decade he was taunted with Fianna Fáil's failure to deliver the promise of full employment. More favourably disposed commentators have pointed to the Clery's speech as the decisive watershed in Lemass's move to switch the Irish economy from protection to free trade. Both sides exaggerate and misinterpret an important speech in his efforts to formulate policy.

Its purpose was made clear in a boldly displayed box on page one of the *Irish Press* and repeated in the introduction to the paper's special supplement, reproducing the full text, published the following morning:

Mr Seán Lemass will tonight initiate a discussion on national development at a meeting of Cómh-Chomhairle Átha Clíath. [93] Fianna Fáil have been engaged for some time on a comprehensive programme for the development of the country's resources ... full discussion by the Fianna Fáil organisation on the proposals will continue until the complete programme, fully outlined and tested in debate, is adopted in final form.

Far from being a fully polished and developed statement, 'Proposals for a Full Employment Policy' was designed by Lemass to cut through the complacency with which his party contemplated inevitable electoral victory and force them to consider a new approach. It was intended to initiate debate in a party which had not questioned its own policy for more than a generation. Its starting point, though far less starkly and bleakly delineated than the opening paragraphs of Whitaker's famous paper, *Economic Development*, was a similar demand for realistic assessment and co-ordinated action.

Had his opponents not been so mesmerised by the spectacular outline of the plan itself they might have seized on this realistic recognition of failure, cloaked in party rhetoric, as a better debating point. Instead they concentrated on the 'promise' of 100,000 jobs. In fact Lemass had been careful to note that restrictive practices might easily compromise the suggested job targets. But overall, it seems fair to accept Dr Whitaker's description of this speech as 'a simple "Keynesian" prescription of increased public investment to generate 100,000 new jobs and provide full employment in five years'.[26] It is also important to stress that, despite the typical assertiveness of Lemass, it was the beginning, not the end, of an argument and to recognise that it served its purpose in stimulating internal debate.

Within a month Lemass engineered an occasion to answer criticism. At a general meeting of the South Central constituency of Fianna Fáil he answered four queries that had been raised.[27] The first — an old charge against Lemass — that the plan placed too much reliance on industry to the neglect of agriculture, was denied. The second, about the vagueness in identifying the direction of state investment, was described as a 'deliberate omission'; what was required was acceptance of the principle, leaving the application in detail to a Fianna Fáil government. The third tackled suspicion about increased government activity in the economic field; Lemass's response was:

> Yes, but there seemed to be no practical alternative. Besides the main aim was to encourage private enterprise and the hope was that it would rise to such a level that the state could 'fade out of the picture.'

Such an attachment to the concept of the mixed economy married to state planning might appear a cyncial evasion of economic consistency but perhaps it reflected something of Lemass's optimistic pragmatism. Certainly he made no bones about dismissing the 'usual stupid comment' — why did Fianna Fáil not do this while they were in office? — with a contemptuous assertion of partisan righteousness. As the *Irish Press* reported:

> They in Fianna Fáil, said Mr Lemass, were not like those beings of whom it was said that they forgot nothing and learned nothing. 'We have face up, in a realistic way, to the fact that the original Fianna Fáil plan has not proved to be comprehensive enough to end unemployment and emigration and that it has now to be extended.'

In fact, even while trying to salvage his party from these pitfalls of total recall that had stultified the Bourbons, instead of extending the economic horizons, Lemass began to pull back. In his plan for 'National Recovery' presented to Cómh-Chomhairle in January 1957 he called for a cut of 5 per cent in personal expenditure either 'voluntarily by saving or involuntarily by taxation' and he also stressed that export growth could not be significantly developed 'without linking up with external firms with ample financial and technical resources and established connections in the world's markets'; even in an election year his message was that only 'a tough, hard road' could lead Ireland out of its economic difficulties.[28] The same thrust was evident in an 'exclusive interview' (more properly 'planted message') in the *Sunday Press* later that month:

temporary measures can only bring temporary relief ...
a permanent cure means more fundamental changes, and [95]
time is running out on us. Patriotism has no higher or more
urgent aim to serve now than getting a start made on the
great effort at economic reorganisation which will ensure
that the country will be able to keep its people.

By this time it was a comment directed as much at Lemass's
own senior colleagues as at the inter-party government, from
whom the withdrawal of Clann na Poblachta support signalled
the end of Fianna Fáil's sojourn in opposition. Lemass, as
director of elections, masterminded the party's campaign
from headquarters. Thanks to his work on organisation and
policy, the 'let's get cracking' slogan worked. Fianna Fáil
with 78 seats achieved its first overall victory since the war;
in his last campaign as leader de Valera was presented with
more seats than ever before. But the composition of the
cabinet indicated the growing influence of Lemass. In 1951
de Valera had refused his request not to reappoint MacEntee
to Finance; in 1957 he acceded.[29]
Indeed by this stage Lemass had gained almost the plenit-
ude of executive power. Although ministers of the time
insist that 'Dev's was still the decisive voice', the old Taoiseach
was much reduced in capacity by age and blindness. He had
neither the inclination nor energy to push policy. Lemass
progressively emerged as the real power behind the throne;
increasingly his department of Industry and Commerce was
the powerhouse within the Irish administrative and governmental structure. Stretching into all the main semi-state
bodies, still retaining responsibilities that would soon demand
independent departmental status, his office in Kildare Street
became a breeding ground for the new generation of public
servants strategically placed in other departments and agencies.
As Tánaiste to the ailing Taoiseach he was in the position to
shape the main thrust of public policy. Economic issues now
displaced the earlier emphasis on constitutional questions and
external relations and Lemass was undisputed master of these
technical briefs. He chaired the cabinet committee which put
the First Programme into final shape,[30] and the task of leading
government, parliament, party and people through the *terra*

incognita of economic planning was left to him. At the 1958 ard fheis it was Lemass who unveiled the government's five-year plan.[31] Yet the promise of future prosperity did little to ease immediate problems. Both emigration and unemployment remained at high levels. There was no sudden awakening to economic reality and opportunity.

The continuing presence of de Valera may have provided Lemass with a convenient cloak of seeming changelessness under which new policies, concerns and choices could be exchanged for old. But there were disadvantages and frustrations in being executive officer rather than captain of the ship of state, especially when the executive wanted economic action and the captain favoured either resting at anchor or setting sail on another political voyage. An astute commentator encapsulated 1958: 'the year was curiously balanced between an encouraging growth of interest in economic policies and, towards its end, a reversion to debates on matters of purely political interest.'[32] Lemass's political energies were to be diverted from economic issues to de Valera's crusade against proportional representation.

Loyalty to his leader and recognition of party advantage left him no choice. There is almost a note of desperation in Lemass's effort to provide an economic justification for the campaign. He argued:

> if the country was to go ahead as rapidly as we wished, it must be certain of maintaining that stability and continuity of economic policy which the straight vote protects and proportional representation endangers.[33]

In fact, he shared de Valera's original preference for the alternative vote in single-seat constituencies and was critical of the Chief's rigidity in rejecting a scheme that would have won both Fine Gael and Fianna Fáil support. He was also critical of de Valera's decision to run for the presidency without relinquishing his position as Taoiseach. It would, Lemass said, have been better both from an electioneering and a party point of view; it would also have relieved his own frustration, as he expressed it, sitting around designated as Taoiseach but neither active nor effective as such. But, as a senior official long and closely associated with de Valera noted, the Chief was reluctant

enough to relinquish power; asked about making arrangements for resignation, he retorted, 'I'm not President yet.' [97]

At the same time there was a deep ambivalence in Lemass's
attitude towards taking over the top post. Like so many
others, he found it difficult, almost impossible, to conceive
of Fianna Fáil without de Valera at the helm. No one yet
knew — few, if any, were prepared to estimate — the likely
effect of the change of leadership on the party's fortunes.
Lemass could not hope to match de Valera's established
electoral appeal; he laid no claim to charisma. He might not
be able to continue to corral the disparate and often divergent
forces within the party. And there was, too, for a man notably
conservative in his personal habits a residual reluctance to
change the familiar life-style of a government minister for
the more sedate role he conceived as appropriate to the
Taoiseach. Yet Lemass's reluctance was counterbalanced
by the realisation — more acutely conscious for him than
others — that de Valera had 'passed the point of no return'
as government and party leader. He had been irritated, from
the beginning of their long political relationship, by his Chief's
tendency to back off decisions when arguments developed.
De Valera sought unanimity: Lemass's whole instinct was
for action. He recognised that the price of agreement could
be delay, the fruit of unity could be stagnancy. He did not
believe in agonising before action and was not worried about
the prospect of making mistakes. He told Michael Mills:

> Generally I would agree that the quick decision is always
> better than the long delayed decision. My own personal
> experience was that once you had some clear concept of a
> problem that you rarely added to your wisdom by going
> back and looking at it again and again, delaying the decision.
> You are just as likely to make mistakes taking the proper
> decisions as taking the delayed decision, but at any rate
> if you have a flexibility of mind you can make adjustments.

Seán Lemass was about to make his greatest political
adjustment. He had progressed from gunman to politician,
from parliamentarian to minister. On 23 June 1959 he
became Taoiseach.

6
Lemass as Taoiseach

Lemass was sixty when he became Taoiseach. He had been a TD for over thirty years, a minister for more than twenty. He knew what government was about and had a clear idea what he wanted to make it do: to bring the independent Ireland he had helped to liberate into a fuller recognition of the responsibilities and opportunities of that independence in the circumstances of the modern world. It involved not a denial, but a redefinition, of idealism; less a rejection than a re-focusing of traditional political aims. At the end of the debate on the nomination of his first government he told the Dáil:

> Personally, I believe that national progress of any kind depends largely upon an upsurge of patriotism — a revival of patriotism, if you will — directed towards constructive purposes. Patriotism, as I understand it, is a combination of love of country, pride in its history, traditions and culture, and a determination to add to its prestige and achievements.[1]

That was a rare incursion into rhetoric for Lemass. He lacked confidence in his ability to communicate at an emotional as well as a rational level. The magic that de Valera could invoke to bind listeners to himself, the carefully honed phrase with which John F. Kennedy could trigger a response, were not part of his oratorical skills. He knew that his accession to power marked a major departure in Irish politics; after de Valera things would never be the same, nor would Lemass wish it otherwise.

In early speeches he tried to invoke this new mood. His words tended to be acerbic rather than inspiring; the images scornful rather than uplifting; the tone provocative rather than persuasive.[2] He admonished a Fianna Fáil dinner in Limerick to reject the false old image of the Irish as

> a grievance-loving, lachrymose people, not very efficient or interested in modern technology, and resentful of any circumstances which might force us to change our traditional methods of living or working ... the men and women of today are in no mood to harken to Jeremiahs.

He told a *Guardian* correspondent that he would like to get rid of the out-of-date and inaccurate picture of the Irish as a backward-looking, inconsequential, unenterprising people. He commented to the Muintir na Tíre Rural Week about the reappearance of the stage Irishman of the Victorian era:

> Even the BBC television service rarely if ever presents a play about Ireland without the characters moving about in clouds of alcoholic vapour.

But, in a revealing aside in the 1960 Budget debate, he told the Dáil:

> I am not at all sure that the main weakness in the Irish character, if there is any weakness at all, is an undue disposition to be sorry for ourselves. I personally hold the philosophy, which I think applies to nations as well as to individuals, that once you start getting sorry for yourself, you are finished.

He made the point to the Dublin Chamber of Commerce annual dinner that increased economic activity was not enough to turn the tide of emigration and dispel the national mood of despondency it induced. It must be

> supplemented by a wider type of activity in which all elements in the country whose words or acts can influence community thinking must participate, to eradicate what I may call the cause of unnecessary emigration, to relax the social tensions which may encourage it, to start the process of eliminating the habit of it and acceptance of its inevitability, so that young men and women will be conditioned to think first and strive harder to make their livelihoods in Ireland before taking the easier course of emigration.

This was the rhetoric of a man more concerned to stimulate changes yet to be achieved than to proclaim the transition from the era of de Valera to the world of Lemass already accomplished; a man trying to create rather than just reflect a community consensus; a man unsure of the acceptability of his image of Ireland to his contemporaries. It was left to later historians and percipient contemporaries to record that 'it was widely felt that the change was symbolic of a deeper change in the spirit of Irish politics and that it provided an opportunity to reassess policies that had been inherited from the past.'

Superficially, at the level of Dáil politics, it seemed to be business as usual. Major opposition speakers in the debate on the nomination of Taoiseach rehearsed old charges against Lemass.[3] Costello accused him of ignoring the wishes of the people; Blowick and Dillon painted him as an untrustworthy breaker of rash promises; Oliver Flanagan asserted, 'there is no person with a more dishonest public record'; Mulcahy's peroration catalogued a series of defects in the Taoiseach designate:

> lack of complete understanding of where our political strength came from that enabled us to make this establishment what it is, lack of understanding of many of the problems and the magnitude of them, left to the hands of any leader of government today, by reason of the fact that the spirit and intention of this parliament has been trampled on by his party from the time it was established.

Only a few of the younger opposition deputies registered less conventionally partisan points: Lindsay spoke warmly of 'his personal generosity in this country and abroad'; Corish compared him to Anthony Eden and suggested that 'he has not got a fair crack of the whip'; Browne, while critical of his dependence on private enterprise and failure to devise a more equitable society, spoke of his 'solid achievements'; M.J. O'Higgins suggested that the new government might gain support 'if Deputy Lemass takes the decision to have something of a clearing in the ranks of the cabinet and brings in some new blood'.

But Lemass proved cautious in his approach to cabinet-making. Through the later fifties, often at his instigation, de Valera had gradually shed some of the veteran Fianna Fáil ministers, but when he retired in 1959 there were still four of his original 1932 cabinet in office: Lemass, MacEntee, Ryan and Aiken. All were to continue and, ten years later, Lemass recollected how he approached the formation of his first cabinet and commented on the central theme of the relation of Taoiseach and government:

I considered whether I should make Jim Ryan Tánaiste, not because of any personal consideration but because I felt that, in the government as it is, the seniority of the Minister for Finance should be marked in some way. In effect he does sit at the cabinet table in a much stronger position to criticise or to veto proposals of other ministers than even the Taoiseach because every proposal involves finance of some kind. Therefore, his position is quite powerful in the government and I felt that the fact that the Minister for Finance was a little senior to the other ministers should be indicated by the fact that he was appointed Tánaiste, and that he should automatically be Tánaiste. In fact, the Tánaiste's only function is to take the chair at cabinet meetings when the Taoiseach is absent.

MacEntee was the senior minister. It would have seemed a rebuke to him if I did not appoint him as Tánaiste so I did appoint him. It is far more important to maintain goodwill and harmony than seek a more effective distribution of responsibility.

The young men were Boland, Blaney and Jack Lynch in the early stages. It would be a good thing for the government if there were some device by which the opportunity of appointing new men to the cabinet presented itself fairly regularly. This raises the question of the age at which a minister should retire. One of the weaknesses in the cabinet here is that most of its members depend upon their jobs for their livelihood. It is serious for them if they find themselves out of a job. In Britain this problem does not arise; they can give retired ministers posts like that of colonial governor, which gives them income without cabinet membership and even an opportunity of a dignified retirement which could, in some circumstances, be called promotion. We do not have that here.

My view as to the capabilities of individual members of the government would be a personal view but I would certainly have no difficulty in putting them in order of merit and it would be helpful from the point of view of the party if one could be sure of the opportunity of doing this. Young men are coming along in the party now and their mind is set on when they will reach the stage of being in line for consideration for a ministerial appointment. They will feel frustrated if they see men remaining in office whom they feel are less competent than themselves or so old they should be retired. I did not get an opportunity to make any changes at all until 1961. I made changes then, and would have kept on making changes time and again – if for no other reason than to make it quite clear to any new man that if he showed he had ability the road to promotion was fairly open to him.

In fact Lemass did make changes prior to 1961. However, the overall shape of his early team does not correspond to the usually received (and carefully cultivated) impression of the new Taoiseach surrounding himself with bright, energetic, young ministers.[4] He did promote Jack Lynch to his own old portfolio of Industry and Commerce but also announced his intention to hive off responsibility for transport, fuel and power to a new department.[5] He prevailed upon a reluctant Dr Patrick Hillery (then contemplating relinquishing politics in favour of his medical practice in West Clare) to move from the backbenches to the Department of Education. He failed to persuade Seán Ormonde to postpone retirement from government through ill-health[6] and nominated Michael Hilliard to the vacancy in Posts and Telegraphs. A month later he promoted Gerald Bartley from Parliamentary Secretary to be Minister for the Gaeltacht;[7] it was an appointment that came as news to both cabinet and party. It signalled Lemass's determination to retain sole authority for ministerial appointments. At the same time Lemass was more ready than de Valera to sound opinion among trusted colleagues and, in particular, to discuss ministerial appointments with Dr Jim Ryan.

Dillon professed to see a purely electoral calculation in these appointments: there were to be by-elections in both Clare and Meath, hence the appointments of Hillery and Hilliard.[8] Lemass, who did not have to respond to the point, flatly denied the suggestion. He had a considerable opinion of Hillery's ministerial potential and was subsequently to promote him to both Industry and Commerce and to the new Department of Labour. He had had the opportunity to form a view of both Hilliard and Bartley since both had served briefly as parliamentary secretaries in Industry and Commerce. There is no substantial evidence to show that Lemass, although undoubtedly keenly aware of the importance of electoral geography, allowed this consideration to determine the distribution of ministries. Indeed in his last cabinet there were two ministers in both Donegal and in Mayo and two in the same Dublin constituency.

He was also more cautious than might have been expected in creating the much-vaunted 'youngest cabinet in Europe' and less successful than has been recognised in reforming governmental structures. In 1960 when Oscar Traynor requested the assistance of a parliamentary secretary to handle statute law reform, Lemass originally suggested one prominent backbencher. In cabinet his colleagues insisted that the appointment go to C. J. Haughey, a close aide through Cómh-Chomhairle Átha Clíath and his son-in-law. Both men have recalled the interview in which Lemass told Haughey that it was his duty as Taoiseach to convey the government's invitation to become parliamentary secretary and his duty as father-in-law to advise him not to be fool enough to take it. The incident is indicative of Lemass's sensitivity to the possible charge of nepotism. It also illustrates, once again, the marked contrast between the persistent rumours about Lemass (which had been particularly damaging earlier in his career) and the reality.

Haughey had no difficulty in carving out his area of responsibility as parliamentary secretary. Nor, subsequently, was Donagh O'Malley inhibited in handling the virtually independent Board of Works portfolio. But both Brian Lenihan and George Colley had difficulties with their ministers. Lemass as Taoiseach had stated his clear aim and intention to give these parliamentary secretaries defined functions and responsibilities, in effect to be junior ministers for Fisheries and the

104] Gaeltacht. However, he was unable to circumvent the con-
straints of the Ministers and Secretaries Act that made
parliamentary secretaries responsible to their ministers rather
than to the Taoiseach and government. Despite both a desire
and reputation for short-circuiting established procedures in
the interests of executive action, it is clear that in these cases
an individual minister could frustrate Lemass's purposes.[9] On
the other hand it could be argued that no great issue of
policy was at stake and he was willing to leave the young men
to fend for themselves.

Also influencing Lemass in relations with other ministers
were elements in his own personality and experience: a certain
conservatism that was comfortable with men he knew and
could manage, a lack of that political ruthlessness, that taste
for butchery, that has allegedly characterised modern British
prime ministers. He told Michael Mills:

> I was always reluctant to contemplate change because you
> get in the habit of working with the same set of people,
> you know how to handle them, you know how to get
> results out of them. With newcomers, no matter how well
> you think you know them, there is always a bit of a prob-
> lem. I don't think that I, as Taoiseach, could have done
> what say Macmillan did, sack half his government in one
> day and appoint a new lot of ministers in their stead.

This did not prevent him acting decisively when challenged
directly. Several times he ignored threats of resignation from
Paddy Smith, Minister for Agriculture.[10] Smith, a founder
member of Fianna Fáil, shared a common rural suspicion of
Lemass. The Taoiseach deflected trouble by advising his
colleague, when in a resigning mood, to sleep on it. In
October 1964 matters came to a head when Smith objected
to the settlement of an eight-week long building strike as a
surrender to 'not only a tyranny but a dishonest, incompetent
one'. Lemass was well prepared to act; he was conscious that
Smith's temperament had ruffled the ordinary party members
as well as cabinet colleagues, confident that he would neither
provoke a revolt nor resign his seat. When Smith released news
of his resignation to the newspapers, Lemass recaptured the

initiative by moving Haughey into Agriculture. It was that news rather than Smith's resignation which dominated the papers on the next day.

The resignation occurred during the recess and on the Dáil resumption Lemass announced two further changes: the promotion of Brian Lenihan as Minister of Justice and the nomination of George Colley as parliamentary secretary.[11] Six months later, following the 1965 general election, Lemass completed the task of governmental rejuvenation. Ryan, MacEntee, and Bartley had all gone. Only Aiken remained with Lemass as survivors of the original 1932 Fianna Fáil cabinet. Without consulting the government, he also named six new men as proposed parliamentary secretaries.[12] It is a measure of Lemass's acceptance by the Dáil and his success in effecting the transition of a new generation into office that the debates on the nomination of Taoiseach and of government were both extremely short; in each case, even allowing for a division, the proceedings took only forty minutes.

Lemass introduced a new style into the relations between Taoiseach and ministers. He not only recruited much younger men to replace his own near contemporaries, he encouraged them to develop their own policy initiatives and their own reputations. In part this was a healthy antidote to the apparently monolithic Fianna Fáil of de Valera; in part, an essential contribution to his scheme to convert the staid public service departments into developmental corporations; in part, a deliberate attempt to stimulate a higher degree of ministerial achievement by healthy professional rivalry and competition. One result was a far more lively, personalised and colourful approach to political commentary and reporting. Young ministers were ready to trade information for publicity, to exchange inside gossip for coverage. Lemass did not object. He himself was an adroit exploiter of the inspired leak, willing to organise press speculation on matters of concern, able to mobilise popular support as a means of accelerating executive action. He regarded this, as he told Michael Mills, as

part of the art of political leadership. One of the methods by which a head of a party or the head of a government leads his party along a political line of action is to speak in public in favour of a line of action before the government or party had decided on it. This is a technique very frequently used and, of course, the Taoiseach or leader of a party who did this on a line which was bound to bring him into conflict with the party would be very foolish. But there are many cases where you could not get the decision in principle to proceed in a particular line in reasonable time without in some way committing your colleagues to follow the line.[13]

On occasions he went far beyond this procedure. He was ready to 'plant' a good story, fly a kite in order to test opinion. Sometimes a journalist was used, as when the political correspondent of the *Irish Times* was given and reported exclusive information on a proposed honours list only to have the story denied. Sometimes he was ready to use a ministerial colleague as a front man for a controversial initiative, as when the Minister for Lands was prompted to raise the possibility of Ireland subscribing to NATO in a speech at Claremorris. When the predictable storm erupted on the question and the Minister somewhat plaintively asked what he should do, Lemass's sardonic suggestion was that he should hold a press conference. After the topic was taken up by the newly opened Irish television service Lemass was reluctant to offer a ministerial spokesman. However, when the controversy gave rise to a series of Dáil questions, Lemass handled the matter himself and carefully evaded the issue of whether the speech was approved in advance.[14]

He was similarly evasive when the most celebrated example of policy-making by publicity was perpetrated by Donagh O'Malley. In a rapidly advancing ministerial career, first in the Board of Works and subsequently in the Department of Health, O'Malley had gained a reputation for 'leapfrogging' the legitimate claims and objections of other departments by announcing new policies. In his maiden speech as Minister for Education to the National Union of Journalists in September 1966 he announced:

I propose from the coming school year, beginning in September of next year, to introduce a scheme whereby up to the completion of the Intermediate Certificate course, the opportunity for free post-primary education will be [107] available to all families.

The announcement was greeted enthusiastically. But there had been no proper governmental consultation, let alone any formal decision on the matter. In particular Lynch, Minister for Finance, who was not in the country at the time of the announcement, was affronted at this cavalier disregard of procedure and raised the matter in cabinet. However, it appears that the Taoiseach refused to be drawn into the matter. But there is evidence to indicate that Lemass had seen and even amended the text in advance; more precisely, five members of that cabinet have separately told the present author that they believed Lemass had seen the speech before delivery. That belief itself is an interesting indication of his colleagues' perception of Lemass's attitude to cabinet procedure.

Certainly he was determined to avoid the long-winded and repetitive discussions that had characterised de Valera's style of cabinet chairmanship. He was conscious of the contrast:

He had a different technique to mine. He relied upon the force of physical exhaustion to get agreement. In other words he'd never let a cabinet debate on any subject end with a vote of ministers.

He always wanted to get unanimity and he sought this unanimity by the simple process of keeping the debate going — often till the small hours of the morning, until those who were in the minority, out of sheer exhaustion, conceded the case made by the majority. This technique was quite effective in his case. It's one that I wouldn't have the patience to apply: so, as head of the government, I made a personal judgment as to the point in the debate at which the question had to be put for decision to the government. At that stage you had a fairly good idea what the decision was going to be anyway.[15]

Lemass was far more business-like in cabinet: he liked meetings to finish, as well as to start, on time; he was not averse to putting matters to the vote. He was also adept at resolving inter-departmental and inter-ministerial disputes prior to formal cabinets and was sufficiently senior and dominant to secure his own way on all major decisions.

But for all his brusque executive style and his skill in orchestrating cabinet discussion to an abrupt and decisive climax, Lemass was not a dictator. He still had to endure some ministers who pursued an argument long after it was lost. He was sufficiently interested in the flow of ideas to recognise that the old rectangular cabinet table inhibited communication and to replace it with a cigar-shaped table that enabled all to see and hear a speaker. He took some pride in telling Michael Mills:

> I can tell you this for sure. I presided over a government in which there were plenty of arguments . . . and presided at party meetings where argument was the rule rather than the exception.

In his first presidential address he told delegates to the Fianna Fáil ard fheis of 1959:

> There are no 'yes' men in the government. Each of them when he has a view to express on some problem gives it clearly and often forcibly. But we have never yet failed to reach agreement in the end and when the decision is taken, we all work as a team to carry it through. That is the kind of government anyone would like to be associated with.

On the other hand senior party critics have argued that he gave his ministers less of a free hand.[16] Certainly he did divert decisions to cabinet committees and was prone to phone ministers directly to probe for action. A senior minister recalled a terse personal phone call from Lemass telling him to have a paper ready for the cabinet in two days and commented that 'Dev had a different way of doing things.' At least one new entrant to the cabinet in 1965 has suggested that by the time the younger men arrived Lemass was so senior and so experienced that they were ready to defer to him. Other young ministers report that he did not interfere with the way they handled their departmental briefs. One commented that 'he expected you to know your brief, he expected you to fight for it and very often he would oppose you and so make sure that you knew what you were at, what you wanted and that it was quite certain you wanted it.'

Perhaps these differing perceptions merely reflect Lemass's pragmatic view that the Taoiseach deals with his ministers on the basis of his knowledge of their personalities: some required prodding, others needed support, others could be given their heads. In his own judgment he did attempt to exercise greater supervision over what was going on within each department, not to limit its freedom but to avoid contradictions in the general direction of government policy. In his own words:

> A minister is supposed to know everything about the affairs of his department; the Taoiseach is supposed to know something about the affairs of every department. The Taoiseach's primary task, apart from acting as spokesman for the government on major issues of policy, is to ensure that departmental plans are fully co-ordinated; that the inevitable conflicts between departments are resolved, that cabinet decisions are facilitated and that the implications of government policy are fully understood by all cabinet colleagues and influence the shaping of their departmental plans.[17]

Undoubtedly his capacity to master a brief quickly and his discipline in reading his papers gave extra assurance to his command of even this unduly restricted view of the Taoiseach's functions. But, in fact, he had a wider view of the office.

There was little doubt about Lemass's pre-eminent position. He was not a man content to see the role of Taoiseach as *primus inter pares*. He saw himself as the man in the driving seat and was determined to direct the government and the country to its overdue rendezvous with the realities of the later twentieth-century world. Up to the time of his accession, despite his immense influence, his authority could be challenged. Now, for the first time, he was in a position to put his foot down on the accelerator and get things moving more rapidly. He had already determined the direction of the journey: away from protection and towards free trade. He had already begun to dismantle the tariff barriers he himself had done so much to erect a quarter of a century earlier. Now he began to make further breaches in the walls of Irish economic isolation. As he told the Dáil at the end of the 1959 session:

> I believe we have settled the main features of our policy in a way which gives results. That policy is not carved upon stone. We are prepared to extend and improve it whenever the opportunity of doing so presents itself.[18]

The policy was, of course, that laid down in the First Programme. It involved increased state expenditure in what were designated productive investment areas, an effort to push up both agricultural and industrial production and exports, the encouragement of adaptation by Irish industry and of foreign investment in Ireland, and a major overhaul of Ireland's overseas trading arrangements. Initially this involved not only efforts to accommodate Irish needs to the conditions being demanded both by EEC and EFTA but also the negotiation of a new agreement with Britain. Subsequently he was to regret the amount of time and energy which he devoted to the abortive negotiations for a European Free Trade Area and the impression created by Irish demands for special concessions which later raised doubts about the country's capacity to assume full EEC membership.

But it was a useful learning experience for a man so long accustomed to concentrate on domestic economic issues and the detail of Anglo-Irish trade; it helped to expand his horizons and equip him to act, as in large measure circumstances forced him to do, as the director of Irish foreign policy throughout the greater part of his period as Taoiseach. This involvement by the Taoiseach of the day had longer-term implications for Irish administration; it helped to elevate the role of his department in future negotiations regarding Irish entry into Europe at the expense of the Department of External Affairs. It also helped to provide alternative occupation for a man used to a busy schedule.

Yet there were many temptations to take a personal hand in the execution of domestic policy. There was an element of frustration in being removed from the front line in the struggle to force Irish industry out of the cocoon of protection. He could, and did, give leadership. In a series of speeches he set out to educate and persuade industrialists as well as the general public, politicians as well as civil servants, that new approaches were needed. He encouraged the Federation of Irish Industries to begin the review of industrial prospects under free trade conditions which was to lead to the Committee on Industrial Organisation.[19] Perhaps, above all, he continued to ring the changes on what he had defined as the national aim for the Ireland he was leading: 'the historic task of this generation is to secure the economic foundation of independence.' Still he was above and removed from the immediate scene of the action and he fretted at the loss of this personal involvement. In later years he contrasted the contentment and satisfaction of his years in Industry and Commerce, when 'the office was the office and its problems could wait till next morning,' with the ceaseless and diffuse worries that sprang up for him as Taoiseach with every morning's newspaper.

None of this showed on the surface. To his staff he appeared his somewhat gruff, workmanlike self, regular in arriving at the office about 9.40 and leaving promptly at 5.25. They noted his alacrity in handling papers; a newly arrived file would be in his 'Out' tray within a half-hour, accompanied where necessary by a curt note recording a decision. Notes outlining themes for a speech were scribbled on a page, typed up and then reworked by Lemass himself. Those who had worked close to de Valera were most conscious of the change: with the Chief they had been almost part of the family; under the Boss they were part of a machine. There was no chatting over the events of the day; no stream of welcome American visitors in the summer months. They noted an almost ruthless disregard for time-wasting: when his own son sought an audience on a constituency matter he was dispatched to the appropriate minister; when a parliamentary secretary insisted he receive a visitor, he responded testily 'why doesn't he see him himself?' Normally extremely cool and composed, he was capable of showing anger – or, as one shrewd senior civil servant suggested, of simulating anger. Typically he appeared reserved, controlled, detached. Only a trained observer noted the small occasional sign of strain at the cabinet table: the deeper breathing or, later on, an oedema around the mouth. But this might simply have been the price of a lifetime of self-discipline. Certainly the over-riding impression created was of a man full of ideas, energy and innovation.

To some extent the concentration on Lemass in terms of his pragmatism and central concern for economic policy have obscured his contribution in other areas. Through the late 1950s and especially the early 1960s under a succession of younger ministers — Lynch, Hillery, O'Malley — there was what has been described as an 'almost bewildering number of developments in official policy' on education.[20] The constant element was Lemass: it was he who nominated the ministers and supported them in their struggles against bureaucratic, ecclesiastical and cultural vested interests; it was he who smoothed the path for a massive increase in state expenditure on education. He shared to a considerable extent the contemporary practical emphasis on the contribution of education to economic growth implicit in the OECD sponsored report, *Investment in Education*; he was also conscious, as an early school-leaver himself, of the need to provide more equal access to education for children of all classes. Behind the apparent hard-faced man of affairs lurked an educational reformer.

Similarly his most quoted remark about broadcasting gives an erroneous impression of heavy handed censorship. Lemass's description of RTE as 'set up by legislation as an instrument of public policy'[21] provoked considerable controversy about the relationship of government and broadcasting. Yet his period in office saw the formal establishment of RTE under a Broadcasting Act clearly modelled on the Charter of the BBC and witnessed the development of a range of independently structured, probing and outspoken programmes. Conflict with politicians arose precisely because broadcasting had been given the facilities, money and freedom to develop under Lemass. There were many aspects of these developments which he disliked, not least the predominance of radical minority views among broadcasters, but the real struggle to muzzle the growing communication giant took place after his time.

Perhaps the most startling action of Lemass as Taoiseach was his decision to visit Terence O'Neill, the prime minister of Northern Ireland, at Stormont Castle. The event itself was momentous. It revealed to many a new facet of a man so long characterised simply as managing director of Ireland Inc. Indeed one of the criticisms made on his nomination as Taoiseach was that 'he never makes any statements about partition . . . it seems he has little interest in partition.'[22] It was a common enough misreading of Lemass's public reticence for indifference. While he served under de Valera he left it to the Chief to make the speeches. But he had his own strong views both on the issue and the solution.

The starting point was a fervent nationalism, rarely expressed, masked by the image of the calculating man of affairs, but always central to Lemass. It sometimes broke through, as Seán MacEntee has reported:

> There were occasions, admittedly rare, when, as with a polar volcano, the ice-cap rent itself to expose the heart of fire and ancient resentment that burned within . . . and then his colleagues at the cabinet table caught a glimpse of his innermost feelings. And on these occasions they were hard and dour, almost one might have thought, implacable.

Certainly Lemass never yielded in negotiations with the British. An internal minute records an exchange in the course of a 1947 discussion on coal supplies to Ireland. Northern Ireland was given an allocation; no provision was made for the South. The British argued that they had an obligation to supply the North as part of the United Kingdom:

> the Tánaiste contended that the temporary occupation of part of Ireland by Britain was scarcely sufficient justification for the disparity of treatment between the two parts of the country.[23]

If, in part, this was a negotiating tactic, it also revealed the persistence of Lemass's conviction that the border was an unjustly imposed and essentially temporary expedient by Britain to resolve a political difficulty. He became more convinced in the post-war period that British politicians and officials were embarrassed by the anomaly of Northern Ireland and would be glad to be rid of this colonial encumbrance. He also accepted that Britain could not initiate any proposal to withdraw until there was some resolution of internal

Irish differences both between North and South and between the two communities within the North.

Already, as Minister for Industry and Commerce, Lemass had been involved in cross-border negotiations. He had concluded the agreement on the joint operation of the Great Northern Railway in Belfast and initiated the later agreement on the Foyle fisheries. He saw in such practical, technical arrangements the first tentative steps towards an eventual political agreement. He recognised increasing ministerial cross-border contacts as an important advance on the Cold War mentality of traditional anti-partition propaganda. He linked the cause of national unity with that of economic development, arguing as early as 1953 that the main governmental pre-occupation of reconstructing the national economy and raising the living standards of the Irish people was hampered by partition and hinted that a united Ireland might subscribe to NATO.[24]

Before he became Taoiseach he was already convinced that efforts to coerce or compel the Unionists into a united Ireland were futile and was ready to contemplate some sort of federal solution that might reassure them. In his speech concluding the debate on the nomination of government he made the point that

the problem of restoring national unity is, in essence, one of breaking down the barriers of suspicion, antagonism, prejudice and misunderstanding which now divide a minority in the north east from their fellow countrymen. Anything which tends to break or lower these barriers is good; anything which tends to raise or strengthen them is bad. I think it is as simple as that, and certainly that outlook will continue to settle our policy and determine our actions.[25]

He had already made a start by choosing Belfast as the location for an address on EFTA.

In the next few years Lemass worked to translate his revisionist policy on the North into practical politics. He discouraged the constant use of the United Nations as a forum for anti-partitionist propaganda; discontinued gradually the pejorative term 'six counties' in favour of 'Northern Ireland'; continued to hint that a united Ireland might moderate its neutrality.[26] He went out of his way to exhibit both his interest in and flexibility towards a resolution of the unity issue. In an interview with the *Belfast Telegraph* he suggested that 'the economic problems of both parts of the country derive from the same sources ... they will yield more readily to action on a nation-wide basis' and revived de Valera's plan for the continuance of Stormont with Westminster functions transferred to an All-Ireland parliament. His first message as Taoiseach to the annual conference of the Anti-Partition League held in Manchester urged 'patience, tact and goodwill'. In a speech to the Oxford Union, published as a pamphlet entitled *One Nation*, he developed these arguments at some length, urging again that Irish unity was in the best interest of both islands and suggesting that 'the removal of partition would make possible a fresh approach to consideration of the place of a reunited Ireland in the scheme of western defence.'

These attempts to shift public opinion in Britain and the North had their effect on domestic opinion in the South, not least within Fianna Fáil itself. This may have prompted him to invoke an IRA statement of 1923 in a Dáil debate of 1960 to justify the theoretical case for majority rule but he still reiterated the view expressed at Oxford:

is it not plain common sense that the two existing political communities in our small island should seek every opportunity of working together in practical matters for their mutual and common good?[27]

As the upturn in the economy became more obvious he challenged the Unionists in the North to compare 'their despondence' within a still unreconstructed economy and the optimism generated by the early success of economic planning in the South:

we are showing that freedom is not a barrier but an aid to economic advancement ... the men of the North cannot be unattracted by the concept of self-reliance, the virtue of solving one's problems by one's own efforts. We are proving that there are better ways of dealing with this country's problems than by sending deputations to plead for help from others. The bread of charity is never very filling.

It was a shrewd thrust. But, as a political realist, he recognised
that Stormont was not yet ready to change, even if there was
the beginning of a formless movement of general public
opinion:

> the situation [in the North] does not encourage normal
> political criticism, but I do not believe that any body of
> reasonable people can be kept inarticulate for ever by the
> repetition of out-of-date slogans.[28]

And in a brief interview on BBC Television Northern Ireland,
he repeated his belief that 'the political implications of the
border will diminish very considerably when we are all in the
European Free Trade Area'.

Against this background it was easy for Lemass to respond
to the prospect of change in the North on the accession of
O'Neill. Asked about the possibility of a meeting with the
Northern prime minister he first repeated a 'willingness to
meet at any level and without any preconditions' and then
explicitly stated

> I do not think there can be any misunderstanding regarding
> my willingness to meet the prime minister at any time to
> discuss practical problems of common interest and methods
> of co-operation to solve them and I would welcome an
> indication that Captain O'Neill would be prepared to talk
> over such matters.[29]

It was as good as an invitation. The decision was more difficult
for O'Neill. The Northern prime minister was operating under
considerable pressure and this seems to have coloured his
account of the meeting; the following summary attempts to
reconstruct the circumstances more accurately.

The major contact between the two sides was made at the
level of senior officials. The northern background of T. K.
Whitaker, Secretary of the Department of Finance, made it
easier for him to establish a relationship with the Northern
prime minister at World Bank meetings. Transatlantic crossings
brought him in closer contact with Jim Malley, O'Neill's
private secretary. Each official was a trusted confidant of his
principal; each shared their appreciation of the value of a
formal meeting. When Malley came secretly to Whitaker in

Dublin with an informal invitation and asked for an immediate response he was sent to look at the pictures in the
National Gallery. Lemass quickly agreed to a meeting but
was prevailed upon to consult the Minister for External
Affairs. Aiken hummed and hawed but Lemass's mind was
made up. After all he had already prepared opinion for his
more open approach to the North; when Michael Mills asked
if he had any worries about reaction the response was
unequivocal:

> No. None at all. I knew that people down here would
> regard this as a breakthrough, the first occasion since
> partition that we appeared to be moving together. I knew
> at the time that O'Neill was going to have a problem.

This awareness may have been responsible for the curious
incident at the meeting recorded by O'Neill. According to his
account, Lemass gave no reply to his carefully phrased and
rehearsed greeting, 'Welcome to the North'. It was only when
invited to use the spacious facilities of Stormont House that
in the privacy of the lavatory he uttered his first words: 'I
shall get into terrible trouble for this.' Those who knew
Lemass's laconic ways would not be surprised at the lack of
greeting; those who knew him better might suspect the opening gambit as a device to share experience with the respondent
who answered realistically: 'No, Mr Lemass, it is I who will
get into trouble for this.' So it proved. Yet this and the subsequent return meeting in Dublin, as well as a meeting with
the Northern Nationalist leader, Eddie McAteer, in which
Lemass encouraged his party to participate in Stormont, were
brave efforts to break the historic logjam of Irish politics. On
his return to Dublin after the momentous and successful
meeting which had captured imaginations and headlines, the
Taoiseach was asked for a statement to the press; cool as ever,
he said simply, 'tell them things will never be the same.'
    It might serve as an epigram for his whole conduct as
Taoiseach. He saw his role, in a phrase of the perceptive *Irish
Times* editorial on his death, as 'a mould-breaker and a
mould-maker'.[30] It spilled beyond the confines of domestic
and cross-border policy into international affairs. Since Fianna
Fáil's return to office in 1957 he had been the government's

principal spokesman on European affairs and handled all questions of Ireland's relations with EFTA and the EEC.[31] Following the 1961 general election he answered a question about the conduct of the Irish application to the EEC explicitly: 'I think the main responsibility for these negotiations must rest on myself as Taoiseach', and he continued to exercise that responsibility . But, with Aiken mainly concerned with Irish representation at the United Nations, Lemass took on a wider role. Starting from his original special interest in the economic and trading aspects of foreign policy, 'he became considerably involved in the evolution of policies' and, in the extended absences of the Minister in New York, even in the administration of the department.

Although de Valera had retained direct responsibility in foreign affairs for most of his period as Taoiseach and had acquired a reputation as an internationalist in the League of Nations period, he thought small nations should avoid commitments to international organisations. Lemass thought that position inappropriate in the circumstances of the postwar world and spoke in favour of effective international institutional co-operation at the Paris conference of 1947 preceding the establishment of Marshal Aid. He had none of de Valera's inhibitions about EEC membership.

When the question arose of sending an Irish contingent to join the UN forces in the Congo he had no doubts.[32] The invitation provided an opportunity to demonstrate both the reality and value of an independent Ireland. There was disagreement among senior ministers. MacEntee argued that Lumumba was a communist and that Irish troops in the UN force would be on the wrong side. Aiken, despite his own strong UN commitments, had reservations. Ryan voiced the usual Finance fears of extra financial burdens. On the other hand, the Department of Defence was enthusiastic, there was a clear majority in the cabinet and Lemass was determined to have his way, even if it meant a ministerial resignation. There was no further trouble and when Lemass introduced the enabling legislation in the Dáil it was carried through all stages speedily.

However both in foreign and domestic affairs his principal concentration continued to be on economic issues. For contemporaries as well as for most subsequent historians Lemass was identified with the rising tide of Irish economic growth in the 1960s, at once cause and symbol of the new Ireland developing into prosperity and modernisation as the First Programme surpassed its targets. Every economic indicator was positive. More importantly the century-long demographic decline was reversed. How much of all of this was attributable to Lemass's own efforts, how much the happy coincidence of a politician richly endowed with *fortuna,* how much it may be reduced by revisionist scrutiny is yet to be determined.[33] It may be suggested that there were contradictions and inconsistencies in Lemass's application of economic theory to Irish circumstances. It is certain that the rhetoric of shared prosperity in which the rising tide raised all boats was challenged by continuing structural unemployment and other evidence of widespread relative social deprivation. But there was no mistaking Lemass's intention: he sought to bring Ireland to terms with the realities of the modern world; he bent all his energetic pragmatism to that task.

At the close of the summer session in August 1961, he had indicated early autumn as a likely time for a general election, had emphasised the need for 'change and innovation in every sphere of national activity' and confessed, 'I find the prospect exciting and stimulating.' He proclaimed his credo for the 1960s:

The nation just cannot afford any woolly thinking, any failure of leadership, any slipshod estimating of possibilities and problems, either in the Dáil, in the government, or in any of the organisations within the state to which important sections of our people look for their guidance. We must all look with cold objectivity on the national assets and the national deficiencies so that we can plan properly together to exploit the one and remedy the other.

We know that the country, in its present stage of development, is not as well organised as many other countries to cope with the new situation. That means that we will have to move faster than the others and work hard to catch up with them. That is something we can do. We know that the country's limited size, its geographical location and island character impose some economic handicaps on it. Probably they give us some economic advantages also. The handicaps can only be overcome, as I think everybody now agrees, by making maximum efficiency the objective in every sector, in production, in transport and in management. All that is within our capacity.[34]

It was an appropriate prologue for a general election. Lemass was conscious that he had become Taoiseach by inheritance; there had been no opportunity to gauge the level of his personal support either in the party or the country. He had determined to secure a personal mandate during 1961 and contemplated August as a suitable month for an election. However a breakdown in ESB industrial relations forced a postponement; Lemass had to recall the Dáil on 1 September to enact special legislation to deal with a threatened breakdown of the power supply. Despite his moderation in piloting the legislation through the Dáil, it provoked the all-out opposition of the trade union movement.[35] It was not a happy overture to a campaign but the day after the strike was settled Lemass asked the President to dissolve the Dáil. Immediately he was confronted with another crisis that could have forced a postponement: that same night the Minister for Defence reported a rumoured massacre of 150 troops in the Congo. The dilemma was intensified by the belief that most casualties came from the Athlone garrison; the town chosen by Lemass to begin his campaign. In the event the story was unfounded. However, none of this provided a helpful background to Fianna Fáil's first general election without de Valera.

By 1961 all three major parties had new leaders. Both Fine Gael and Labour gained support, but even Lemass's best efforts failed to secure a majority for Fianna Fáil. Some of the decline may have been due to the absence of de Valera. Some arose from rural suspicions of Lemass; some from loss of support among organised workers. But it is worth noting that in successive general elections from 1927 to 1973 Fianna Fáil zig-zagged from increased to decreased support; on the basis of this pattern, following the 1957 success, it was due to decline in 1961. That was little comfort for Lemass. He was forced to form and maintain a government based on the support of independent deputies. Much praise has been showered on what John Healy ('Backbencher' in the *Irish* *Times*) has characterised as Lemass's 'overall minority' government. For a Taoiseach whose whole instinct was for decisive action it created a nagging political problem. It also prompted speculation – among supporters as well as opponents – that some of his policy shifts and outspoken speeches were tactical responses to political necessity rather than parts of a grand strategic design. Some of this is explicit in contemporary political comment and Dáil debate. The evidence is scarcely compelling. As a committed party man and an experienced politician, Lemass had a low opinion of independent deputies and believed that they would normally vote with a government in order to avoid an election. On the other hand the lack of an overall majority influenced his cautious approach to cabinet rejuvenation; he felt he could not afford to fall out with anyone.

More serious is the charge, especially in regard to the wage settlements, that Lemass was willing to sacrifice economic good sense on the altar of electoral necessity. Some of this is implicit in Smith's letter of resignation.[36] It was a constant theme in opposition speeches. In particular it was alleged that decisions on the 1964 national wage agreement were dictated by Lemass's determination to win two forthcoming by-elections. It is certainly true that he took an active part in the negotiation and suggested a 12 per cent figure which was considerably greater than the employers' opening offer of 8 per cent, let alone the recommendation of a wages stand-still in the government's own White Paper of 1963.

In fact, while Lemass may have been cavalier in arriving at such a figure, it was a reflection of a number of constant features in his approach to settlements. He tended to have what MacEntee called 'a strong bias in favour of the worker and organised labour'.[37] He had always favoured firm decisions rather than uncertainty and believed that the employers would eventually capitulate. He justified a higher settlement within his own department on the grounds that it would help to sort out efficient, thriving firms from declining industries. Perhaps, above all, the settlement reflected his fixed aversion to the waste involved in strikes. It was this which prompted his efforts to promote a better organised and unified trade union movement as well as to create a separate Department of Labour.

Certainly there is much on the record to illustrate Lemass's willingness to court unpopularity. The 1963 White Paper, 'Closing the Gap', is one case in point.[38] Perhaps the most obvious example was the introduction of the 2½ per cent turnover tax in the 1963 Budget. While much of the credit for securing a smooth parliamentary passage of the measure must go to Ryan's shrewd handling, responsibility for committing a minority government to the measure was Lemass's. It was he who launched the first public debate on the proposed move to a new form of indirect taxation in a speech to the Limerick Chamber of Commerce and tried to make it more palatable by arguing that it was a necessary part of a general Budget strategy designed to shift the national policy to the left. And, when he judged the time right, Lemass was not afraid to challenge the voters in the Mid-Cork by-election to either support the government or precipitate a general election.

When they ignored the threat and returned Eileen Desmond in 1965 he did not wait for her to take a seat. The circumstances suited Fianna Fáil: 1964 had been a good year and its Budget, designed to meet the need of farmers, recognised the traditional agricultural support for the party. While industrial relations continued to cause serious problems, Lemass anticipated further trouble ahead in 1966. As things stood he had substantial political advantages, not least his Northern initiative, the imminent creation of an Anglo-Irish Free Trade area, and the return of Roger Casement's remains. Fianna Fáil picked up most of the votes lost in the previous general election and, with exactly half the Dáil seats, Lemass was returned to power and named his 'youngest cabinet in Europe'.

By now he was conscious of age. He had suffered one or two blackouts and was feeling the strain of office. He had accomplished much and, while there was no evidence of failing powers, was ready to make way for a successor. The appropriate time might have been about mid-term but, once he gave an indication of his intention, the succession race took on a pace of its own. Lemass appears to have made little effort to influence the outcome and has frequently been [123] criticised for allowing a divisive contest to develop. He subsequently justified his decision not to 'groom a successor':

this can cause difficulties. If the Taoiseach begins to indicate whom he wants as successor then, of course, it could be discouraging to a lot of people who felt that they could grow to take the office. This is a very difficult decision to take; to sort of indicate who was going to be the choice of the retiring Taoiseach as successor, because everybody's entitled to feel the office is open to him, providing he works hard enough, providing he's good enough.

There may well have been more to it that than. Apart from a broader general belief in the virtue of competition, Lemass had been conscious of the disadvantages of his own unopposed succession. It is known that he 'encouraged' George Colley (who only became a minister in 1965) to think of himself as a potential Taoiseach and act accordingly. It is also clear that Lemass initiated much of the press speculation on candidates during 1966 and reasonable to assume that, as on previous occasions, he contrived to see that certain names were given prominence. When Lynch emerged as an agreed candidate Lemass took a hand in attempting to persuade the other candidates to withdraw.

He himself wanted to leave office with a minimum of fuss, ceremony or sentimentality. A formal statement was distributed; he told a crowded press conference, 'you can take it as read.' Then for over half an hour he handled the usual cut-and-thrust of the press conference. As the *Irish Press* reported:

Only after the searching barrage of questions, encompassing every aspect of national policy, had concluded did the Taoiseach concede anything to the emotion-charged atmosphere of this unique occasion.

To a standing ovation – a tribute from the big press corps – he rose, visibly affected, waved his hand and quickly walked out the side door.

Seán Lemass slipped easily into the role of elder statesman. He continued to serve as Dáil deputy until 1969. He took a place on the All-Party Committee on the Constitution which he had originally established and played an active role with a former opponent in helping to draft some of its interim recommendations, including the controversial proposals to cover matrimonial breakdown. He was active in the European movement. A succession of business directorships added new interests to his later years and gave him the satisfaction of working to the end of a long and busy life.[39]

That public life, so long in the national limelight, obscured much of the man himself. Behind the cool, even cynical, professional politician there remained a committed nationalist whose ideals, tempered by realism, never lost their edge. He was more humorous, more diffident, more deep than the public image allowed. There were contradictions and hidden depths in this far from the simple man. A partisan who found it difficult to hide his contempt for parties other than his own, he had the capacity to make personal friendships across the professional divide. An accomplished and experienced executive, he gambled on his own instincts in making a thousand decisions. A political loner, he could both give and inspire abiding personal loyalty. A supreme pragmatist, his driving ambition, a little engine that knew no rest, was a commitment to an ideal for Ireland that was far removed from the image of the poets or romantic patriots. No one, perhaps, has expressed the real Lemass better than a man of his own generation, a comrade with whom he worked and fought for the best part of half a century, Seán MacEntee:

> the authentic personality of Seán Lemass centred upon one, fixed nucleus; an abiding, restless, ever active urge to make his country and her people, not only prosperous and peaceful, but of some account in the world as well. Those who did not recognise that this was the source of his abounding, venturous ambition and energy could never understand Seán Lemass.[40]

References

Chapter 1: The Political Apprenticeship (pp.1-15)
1. Conor Cruise O'Brien, '1891-1961' in Conor Cruise O'Brien, ed., *Shaping of Modern Ireland*, Routledge and Kegan Paul 1960, p. 13; James Joyce in R. Ellmann, ed., *Selected Letters of James Joyce*, Faber & Faber, paperback, 1975, p. 163.
2. See M. Mills, 'Seán Lemass looks back', *Irish Press*, 20 Jan.-6 Feb. 1969. Unless otherwise indicated all quotations in this chapter from this source.
3. Quoted in an obituary notice of Seán Lemass, *Bulletin of the Department of Foreign Affairs*, no. 837, 18 June 1971; cf. the issue of *Time*, 12 June 1963, which featured Lemass on the cover, p. 46.
4. Seán Lemass in M. Mills, 1969. In the profile of Lemass by Vincent Browne in *Nusight* magazine, Dec. 1969, p. 82, the employee's name is given as Pat Murphy.
5. This was suggested by Seán Lemass in M. Mills, *op. cit.*, 20 Jan. 1969. The following account of Seán Lemass's Easter Week experiences is compiled from this source, his own article, 'I Remember 1916', *Studies*, 55, 1, Spring 1966, pp. 7-9, and the somewhat more heroic interpretation by Liam C. Skinner, in his essay, 'Seán F. Lemass' in *Politicians by Accident*, Metropolitan Publishing Co., Dublin 1946.
6. Seán Lemass in *Studies, op. cit.*
7. Skinner, *op. cit.*, p. 56.
8. The following account is based on M. Mills; L. Skinner, *op. cit.*; Ernie O'Malley, *The Singing Flame*, Anvil Books 1978; R. Briscoe with A. Hatch, *For the Life of Me*, Longmans 1958, p. 155; C. S. Andrews, *Dublin Made Me*, Mercier Press, 1979, p. 222. Cf. Skinner's description, p. 57, of Lemass during the Truce period: 'he invariably wore a cap, riding breeches and leggings, was clean shaven

[126]

and smoked a pipe'. Also the account of Lemass giving off-duty men signed passes to which he affixed the seal of the Lord Chief Justice of Ireland, in C. Younger, *Ireland's Civil War*, Fontana 1970, p. 319.

9. Sinn Féin Funds Case, Public Record Office, Dublin, File 6, 2B/82/116, notes of an interview with Lemass, 10 Dec. 1943: 'He explained that he had never been actively interested in politics as such before the Civil War and was not a member of the Old Sinn Féin organisation.'

10. The Standing Committee minutes in PRO 2B/82/116, File 22, show he attended his first meeting on 4 Dec. 1923 and was appointed a member of a three-man sub-committee over a complaint in Dublin. He attended virtually weekly until Fianna Fáil members resigned on 29 March 1926. Out of a total of 124 meetings up to the break in that month, Seán Lemass appears to have been absent on only eight occasions. Later references given as SFSC.

11. SFSC meeting, 25 Feb. 1924. The motion was attacking P. Ó Caoimh's criticism of the candidature of Mrs Sheehy-Skeffington on the grounds that she was not an orthodox Catholic and had not been reconciled to the Church. Other references in this paragraph relate to SFSC meetings 3, 13, 21 Mar., 4 Apr. 1924.

12. M. Mills, 21 Jan. 1969: 'After I had been selected as a candidate (I should mention that nobody asked me to be a candidate) I read in the evening papers one evening I had been selected and my first reaction was rather one of indignation that they had done this without asking me. It was only next morning I began to feel a sense of pride at having been selected and I agreed to go forward.'

13. The figures on the first count, in an electorate of approximately 75,000 were:

James O'Mara	15,884
John O'Neill	2,928
Seán Lemass	13,639

Skinner, p. 60 gives the complete count.

14. *Irish Times*, 10 Nov. 1924. Quotation below, *Irish Times*, 18 Nov. 1924.

15. The result was:

Seamus Hughes	16,340
Seán Lemass	17,297

The account in the *Irish Times*, 20 Nov. 1924, noted a considerable number of curiously spoiled votes. The figures do not appear to bear out Lemass's own subsequent contention, reported by Mills, that because of Hughes's known involvement in Oriel House 'some 60 or 70 per cent of Cumann na nGaedheal voters wouldn't go out to vote for him'.

16. On Comhairle na dTeachtaí, see Earl of Longford and T. P. O'Neill, *Eamon de Valera*, Dublin 1970, p. 236; T. P. Ó Néill and P. Ó Fiannachta, *De Valera*, II, Áth Cliath 1970, p. 160.
17. SFSC, 8 Dec. 1924: the three other committees were finance, Irish culture and publicity.
18. SFSC, 2 Mar. 1925; earlier reference to meeting of 2 Feb. 1925.
19. SFSC, 4 May 1925; Seán Lemass was made chairman of a seven-member re-organisation committee for Dublin city and county. It produced its first report within a week and frequently provided material for discussion at committee meetings in subsequent months. Resolution below in SFSC, 7 May 1925.
20. J. Bowyer Bell, *The Secret Army*, Sphere Books 1972, p. 89.
21. P. Pyne, 'The Third Sinn Féin Party: 1923-1926' in *Economic and Social Review*, vol. 1, Nos. 1-2, 1969-70, p. 40.
22. Reference to six articles in *An Phoblacht:*
'Sinn Féin in Dublin. What is wrong with it? A personal view', 18 Sept. 1925.
'New Leaders for Sinn Féin. The coming year', 9 Oct. 1925.
'The Turning Tide. The task before the ard fheis', 23 Oct. 1925.
'The Need of Sinn Féin: a fighting policy', 22 Jan. 1926.
'The Need for Sinn Féin: an immediate objective', 29 Jan. 1926.
'The Will to Win', 5 Feb. 1926.
23. A note in Irish at the end of the standing committee minutes for 1 March 1926 records a further query about why this correspondence was permitted to continue.

Chapter 2: The Parliamentary Journeyman (pp. 16-32)
1. Seán Lemass, interview with author.
2. Derived from much later reminiscences recorded in Michael McInerney, 'The Gerry Boland Story', *Irish Times*, as noted in P. Pyne, *op. cit.*, p. 46.
3. M. McInerney, 'The Name and the Game', *Irish Times* supplement on Fianna Fáil, 19 May 1978. In *Eamon de*

[128] Valera, Irish Times 1976, p.55, McInerney reports de Valera recalling

> I told him, 'It looks as if that is the end for me, Seán. I'm chucking politics altogether.' Lemass retorted, 'But you can't leave us now, Dev. We must go on.'

Cf. 'Ansin, Seán Lemass, fear a d'fhág Sinn Féin in éineacht leis, mhol sé do páirtí nua a bhunú' in T. Ó Néill agus P. Ó Fiannachta, *de Valera*, Cló Morainn 1970, vol. 2, p. 181.

4. T. P. O'Neill, 'Birth of the party', *Irish Press* supplement on Fianna Fáil, 26 May 1976. For a detailed account, see a long letter by Patrick Brennan, a founder member, under the heading 'Founding of Fianna Fáil: the full story,' *Sunday Independent*, 14 Mar. 1976 and McInerney *supra*.

5. Information on income and work as organiser from interview with author.

6. Werner Moss, *Political Parties in the Irish Free State*, Columbia UP 1933, p. 141.

7. Reference to press in Moss, *op. cit.*, p. 146; Lemass-O'Donnell meeting in PROD, SFFC, File 6. See also the McGarrity papers, NLI MS 17,532.

8. See McGarrity papers, NLI: Seán T. O'Kelly to Frank P. Walshe, 1 Sept. 1927, MS 17,656/2 and P. McCartan to McGarrity, 6 Sept. 1927, MS 17,617/4. O'Kelly regretted 'that one person of importance at headquarters was unalterably opposed ... was strong enough to be able to get a majority of the committee to take his view.' McCartan wrote: 'Lemass [*sic*] I understand leads one section of the executive; Dev the other. Lemass was for me. Therefore de Valera opposed me and won.' It was not to be the last time that outsiders misinterpreted the relationship between the two men. T. P. O'Neill in the *Irish Press* supplement noted that Lemass 'never sought to rival his leader'.

9. Comment to author. The early quotation from interview in *Irish Press* supplement, 26 May 1976.

10. J. Fitzgerald-Kenney, Minister for Justice, on Lemass's speech on the Public Safety (Repeal) Bill, 10 Nov. 1927, PDDE 21/1222. In the same debate, W. T. Cosgrave commented on Lemass's contribution: 'he certainly seemed to address himself to the matter in a much finer spirit than that of any of the other members of his party who

spoke', 21/1249. Cf. Lemass's own later remark to the Ceann Comhairle: 'I think you will admit, sir, that it is [129] not usual for me to make any personal reference to any one', 34/510, 3 Apr. 1930. A rare exception were his heated remarks to Seán MacEoin, 35/1294, 18 June 1930.

11. Debate on nomination of President of the Executive Council, PDDE 21/51-56, 11 Oct. 1927.

12. Debate on Defence Forces (Temporary Provisions) Bill, PDDE 21/1465ff., 16 Nov. 1927.

13. PDDE 27/273ff., 15 Nov. 1928. Debate on prisons estimate, PDDE 27/384, 16 Nov. 1928.

14. PDDE 22/1223-2194, 14-30 Mar. 1928. The exchange quoted below took place on the second day, 21 Mar., cols 1614-15.

15. Christmas adjournment debate, PDDE 21/1889-90, 24 Nov. 1927. Later in the same debate, the following exchange took place:
Mr Davin: Deputy Lemass expressed amazement and surprise, and stated that the vitality of the Labour Party had been sapped by their long experience in this House, but, while Deputy Lemass and some of his friends were galavanting around the country, the members of our party were sometimes doing the donkey work which should have been done by members of the Fianna Fáil party.
Mr Lemass: Donkey-work is a good word.

16. PDDE 22/2165, 30 Mar. 1928.

17. PDDE 23/1765ff., 18 May 1928.

18. PDDE 40/81, 14 Oct. 1931. Time motion on Constitution (Amendment No. 17) Bill. The quotation below is from his speech on the financial resolution on the bill, same day, at cols 253ff.

19. PDDE 34/316, 2 Apr. 1930. For later references on this topic, see exchanges at 40/1179, 6 Nov. 1931 (P. McGilligan); 69/1568, 2 Dec. 1937 (J. Dillon) and 69/2156, 10 Dec. 1937 (D. Morrissey).

20. PDDE 23/2169, 30 Mar. 1928.

21. For further attacks see: PDDE 24/543ff., 13 June 1928, where he raises treatment of prisoners on the adjournment; reference to 'descendants of the Plantation soldiery of Cromwell' in attack on Senate at 24/2113, 5 July 1928; attacks on gardaí and Special Branch at 26/1395 and 1675, 1 & 7 Nov. 1928; PQ on Dublin arrests leading to Lemass's allegation on the adjournment that the press was not reporting police harassment, 29/4ff. & 168ff.,

[130]

10 Apr. 1929; question of multiple arrests raised on adjournment, 32/180ff., 23 Oct. 1929.

22. Minister for Education, John Marcus O'Sullivan, PDDE 32/1833, 29 Nov. 1929.

23. PDDE 21/404ff., 26 Oct. 1927.

24. PDDE 22/213-14, 22 Feb. 1928. Cf. 39/1019, 25 June 1931.

25. PDDE 22/922ff. and 1100ff, 7 & 9 March 1928.

26. T. K. Whitaker, 'From Protection to Free Trade – the Irish Experience', *Administration*, 21, 4, Winter 1973, p. 406. But cf. Mulcahy's attack on Lemass, *inf.*, p. 100.

27. PDDE 25/925ff., 19 July 1928. Cf. 35/495.

28. Adjournment debate on Tariff Commission report on flour millers' application, PDDE 23/2293ff., 30 May 1928; motion on Saorstát milling industry, 34/945ff., 10 Apr. 1930. Refs. below are: 2nd stage Appropriations Bill, PDDE 27/622ff., 22 Nov. 1928; PDDE 23/2300, 30 May 1928.

29. In adjournment debate on the price of imported coal, PDDE 33/330, 13 Feb. 1930. Reference below: speech on estimate for Industry and Commerce, PDDE, 30/1350ff., 13 June 1929. Reference to car insurance, 40/1340, 6 Nov. 1930.

30. Speech on second stage of Central Fund Bill, PDDE 22/1646ff., 22 Mar. 1928. Reference below: PDDE 32/467ff., 30 Oct. 1929; 2nd stage Central Fund Bill, PDDE 36/1691, 12 Mar. 1930; Local Government (Dublin) Bill, PDDE 34/831ff., 10 Apr. 1930. Cf. his criticism of unduly limited electoral areas where 'that evil of "ward heeler" develops', 26/189, 11 Oct. 1928, Cork City Management Bill; PDDE 34/1106, 30 Apr. 1930; PDDE 34/1242, 1 May 1930.

31. See M. Moynihan, ed., *Speeches and Statements by Eamon de Valera*, Gill & Macmillan 1980, pp. 153ff.

32. Interview with author.

33. PDDE 35/35ff., 28 May 1930.

34. Letter of 13 January 1930 to de Valera quoted in T. Ó Néill and P. Ó Fiannachta, *De Valera*, Áth Cliath 1970, vol. 2, p. 220. Ref. below, PDDE 35/420ff., vote on the Office of the President, 4 June 1930. The quotations below occur at columns 430 and 431/2.

35. PDDE 21/51, 11 Oct. 1927. References below: PDDE 22/140, 22 Feb. 1928; 24/994 and 991, 20 June 1928; 35/374, 30 May 1930; 30/1252, 12 June 1929; 34/1157,

30 Apr. 1930; 34/1250, 1 May 1930.

36. PDDE 40/2380, 2 Dec. 1931. References below are: [131]
    PDDE 34/318, 2 Apr. 1930; Proposed Wheat Control
    Board, PDDE 32/1579, 27 Nov. 1929; PDDE 40/2379,
    2nd stage Unemployment Relief Bill, 2 Dec. 1931. Cf.
    35/993ff., 12 June 1930; PDDE 36/90, 19 Nov. 1930.
37. Estimates for Dept. of External Affairs, PDDE 34/137,
    26 Mar. 1930. Ref. below: PDDE 22/530, 29 Feb. 1928.

Chapter 3: The Ministerial Tradesman (pp. 33-50)

 1. Séan Lemass quoted in M. Mills, *op. cit.*, 24 Jan. 1969.
 2. Ronan Fanning, *The Irish Department of Finance,
    1922-58*, IPA 1978, p. 258.
 3. Quoted in Desmond Roche, 'John Leydon', *Adminis-
    tration*, Autumn 1979, vol. 27, no. 3. This article and
    Fanning, *op. cit.*, are the major sources for the following
    account of the circumstances of Leydon's appointment.
    For formal appointment see S.2470A. This also shows
    the government rejecting a proposal to pay Leydon an
    extra personal allowance of £300 in 1934.
 4. Seán Lemass quoted in M. Mills, *op. cit.*, 24 Jan. 1969.
 5. R. C. Ferguson, 'Industrial Policy and Organisation',
    in F. C. King, ed., *Public Administration in Ireland*,
    Parkside Press, Dublin n.d., p. 42.
 6. PDDE 42/876-86, 8 June 1932.
 7. SPO CAB 6/29, 23-4 May 1932, S.6286.
 8. Private interview. See also below Seán Lemass's memo
    of 1 November 1932. References below: SPO CAB 6/33,
    6 June 1932, S.6230; SPO CAB 6/28, 20-21 May 1932,
    S.6045 on flour milling.
 9. For establishment of economic committee see SPO CAB
    6/26, 13 May 1932. Minutes in S.6276. Cf. Fanning,
    op. cit., pp. 218-21 for this and following paragraph.
10. PDSE 16/474, 14 Dec. 1932.
11. O Néill and Ó Fiannachta, *op. cit.*, II, p. 253, discussion
    of Lemass's economic memoranda of November 1932 is
    based on Fanning, *op. cit.*, pp. 245ff.
12. SPO S.6242A.
13. References are SPO CAB 6/94, 22 Nov. 1932, cabinet
    approve economic committee actions; interim report
    21 Feb.; final report, 24 May and Lemass's observations,
    29 May 1933, SPO S.6242A; Minister authorised, CAB
    7/41, 2 June 1933; Bill introduced, PDDE 49/1430,
    7 Aug. 1933.

14. For further details on background to the 1933 general election see B. Farrell, *Chairman or Chief? The role of Taoiseach in Irish Government*, Gill and Macmillan 1971, pp. 36-7. An informed private source has since reported de Valera's recollection (supported by material quoted in Farrell *supra*) that he consulted no one before calling the election. The official biographers report that the decision 'was taken by de Valera alone. He sent for each minister individually and informed them of his decision' (Longford and O'Neill, *op. cit.*, p. 287). Quote below from W. Moss, *Political Parties in the Irish Free State*, Columbia UP 1933, p. 192. Table based on data in E. Rumpf and A. C. Hepburn, *Nationalism and Socialism in twentieth-century Ireland*, Liverpool UP 1977.

15. Cf. forthcoming history of the ESB by M. McDowell and M. Manning.

16. U.S. government delegate proposing Lemass, quoted in Skinner, *op. cit.*, p. 66. On protection, cf. Meenan, *op. cit.*, p. 142.

17. The references are SPO CAB 7/104, 16 Jan. 1934; 7/154, 3 July 1934; 7/219, 29 Mar. 1935.

18. Fanning, *op. cit.*, p. 257; cf. Farrell, *op. cit.*, pp. 63-4. On Aiken proposal see SPO S.6327, 23 Oct. 1933. Lemass had been a member of this cabinet committee. This letter gives an interesting insight into Lemass's ideas on using the Volunteers to attract young men away from the IRA.

19. The 1935 case discussed below is found in SPO S.7441 Feb.-Apr. 1935. On 1964 see Farrell, *op. cit.*, pp. 65ff. and *inf.*, pp. 104-5.

20. SPO S.7441B.

21. On Lemass's contribution to the Constituion *inf.*, the references are to SPO S.9715 and S.10160 and the quotation from Longford and O'Neill, *op. cit.*, p. 329.

22. This domestic account is based on conversations with the Lemass family and friends. The quotations are from Kerry McCarthy's interview with Mrs Lemass, *Evening Herald*, Friday, 21 Nov. 1975. For other press interviews with Mrs Lemass, see *Irish Press*, 7 Feb. 1969 and *Nusight*, Dec. 1969.

23. Longford and O'Neill, *op. cit.*, p. 310. The following account of the negotiations and agreement of 1938 is based on the official biographies of de Valera; Fanning, *op. cit.*; and Roche, *op. cit.*, and interviews with Seán Lemass.

24. For Banking Commission see Fanning, *op. cit.*; J. Meenan *op. cit.*, and M. Moynihan, *Currency and Central Banking in* [133] *Ireland 1922-60*, Gill and Macmillan 1975, PDDE 36/220.
25. Moynihan, *op. cit.*, p. 284.
26. On the oil refinery see SPO S.6138 and cabinet decisions. The reference to the Dáil debate is PDDE 72/606ff., 8 July 1938 and 72/1009ff., 20 July 1938. Other information from private sources.

Chapter 4: The Mature Ministerial Craftsman (pp. 51-79)
1. The basic source for this section on the Department of Supplies is the internal 'Record of Activities' compiled by the Department. The document is 152pp. long with twelve appendices adding a further 29pp. Use has also been made of a twelve-part 'Historical Survey 1938-45 (Rationing, Miscellaneous Supplies and Control of Exports)' in the files of the Department of Industry and Commerce. Additional information from SPO and, among secondary sources, D. Roche, 'John Leydon'; Joseph T. Carroll, *Ireland in the War Years 1939-1945*, David and Charles, Newton Abbot 1975; and R. Fanning, *op. cit.*, chap. 8.
2. 'Historical Survey' p. 2, Cf. SPO S.11394, memo from Dept of Industry and Commerce, 14 Apr. 1939, which indicates possible courses of action and estimates some of the costs. The discussion of war risk insurance based on Fanning, *op. cit.*, pp. 339ff.
3. Leydon report quoted in 'Historical Survey', pp. 7-8. It is worth noting that at talks at the Board of Trade at the end of April 1939, 'The Secretary of The Ministry of Commerce, Belfast, happened to be in London and was present at the talks in the Board of Trade. While the value of co-operation between all three governments was accepted it was gathered that Northern Ministers would not favour discussions with Dublin departments.' ('Record', p. 7). Quotations below: PDDE, 77/263, 27 Sept. 1939; PDDE 77/6, 2 Sept. 1939.
4. PDDE 77/191, 27 Sept. 1939. Later references in following paragraphs are: W. T. Cosgrave quotation, col. 350; Corish, 453; Hurley, 559; McGilligan, 506; O'Higgins, 468; de Valera, 574 (all on 29 September 1939). On the change in Justice, see Farrell, *op. cit.*, p. 38.
5. SPO S.8814, Lemass to MacEntee, 6 Feb. 1939, in response to MacEntee-Lemass, 31 Jan. 1939. Each

addressed 'Dear Seán'. Correspondence below in SPO S.11244. Sole item in file is letter from MacEntee to de Valera, 2 May 1939. It is marked 'Seen by Taoiseach 11/5. Cláruigh fé bhráid'.

6. Seán Lemass, interview with author. Ref. below to political opponent is General Mulcahy, UCD Archives, Mulcahy Papers, PI/C/145, 10 Jan, 1940. I am indebted to Professor Maryann Valiulis, La Fayette College, Pa., for this reference.

7. SPO S.11418A, government minute allocating functions to the Department of Supplies.

8. 'Record', p. 49. On this period see D. Roche, *op. cit.*, p. 238. Quotation below from 'Lemass on Government', *Léargas: public affairs review*, no. 12, Jan.-Feb. 1968, pp. 2-4.

9. Cf. e.g., PDDE 81/2451ff., 20 May 1942 where J. A. Costello raised the issue of a reduction in the petrol ration for six prominent Dublin doctors.

10. *Evening Herald*, Mrs Lemass interview, 21 Nov. 1975. Quotation below: M. Mills, *op. cit.*, 25 Jan. 1969.

11. J. Meenan, 'The Irish Economy during the War' in K. B. Nowlan and T. D. Williams, eds, *Ireland in the War Years and After 1939-1951*, Gill and Macmillan 1969, p. 31. Lemass's own view below is quoted from Mills, *op. cit.*, 25 Jan. 1969.

12. This discussion of the background to the 1940 trade talks is based on SPO S.11846A.

13. I am indebted to Dr Paul Bew for drawing my attention to the following minute by Lord Rugby of a meeting with de Valera on 16 October 1947 (ref. PRO London Prem 8/824):

Lord Rugby to de Valera.

I then said, 'Do you mean to say that if you were paying an official visit to London and that the King was there, you would not pay the call which custom and courtesy require?' Mr de Valera said, 'In my present circumstances I could not. Any such action on my part would be open to grave misinterpretation in this country.' I lifted my eyes in astonishment at this and said, 'Well, in this country the tail does wag the dog! When international courtesy is in issue the country would look to you for its proper interpretation and be entitled to get it.' Mr de Valera said, 'It has never been done.' (I did not tell him that Mr Lemass

and Dr Ryan, two of his ministers, had called at the Palace moved thereto by me, in May 1940 with his consent.) [135]
Extensive enquiries from Irish sources have failed to un-cover any support for this story.

14. Government decision on 9 July 1940, SPO GC 2/186 (S.11980) and plans supplied 19 July GC 2/189. See also 'Record', p. 25 and pp. 57-61 for details of arrangements.

15. For a fuller account see B. Farrell, 'De Valera: unique dictator or charismatic chairman?' in J. P. O'Carroll and J. A. Murphy, eds., *De Valera and his Times: Political Development in the Republic of Ireland*, Cork University Press, forthcoming.

16. Commission on Emigration and Other Population Prob-lems 1948-54, *Reports*, Dublin, The Stationery Office, 6,472.

17. Records of this committee in SPO S.11903.

18. PRO S.11402B, handwritten letter of Ryan to Taoiseach, 13 Jan. 1941 notes that the minister had raised the matter at the last government meeting. For government decision see GC 2/246, 28 Feb. 1941. Files of the committee in SPO S.12308.

19. *Evening Herald*, Mrs Lemass interview, 21 Nov. 1975. The question of Ruttledge's resignation from Local Govern-ment was raised by J. Dillon, TD on an adjournment motion, PDDE 84/2548ff., 17 Sept. 1941. See also Farrell, *Chairman or Chief?*, p. 38. Quotation below from T. K. Whitaker, 'From Protection to Free Trade — the Irish Experience', *Administration*, 21,4, Winter 1973, p.413.

20. D. Roche, 'John Leydon', *Administration'* 27, 3, Autumn 1979, p.239. Cf. e.g., B. Chubb & P. Lynch eds, *Economic Planning and Development*, IPA Dublin 1969, and R. Fanning, *The Irish Department of Finance*, chapter 11, 'The Emergence of Planning'.

21. SPO S.12882. Government decision in G2/372.

22. Fanning, *op. cit.*, p. 352. For earlier references see PDDE 91/220, 2 July 1943 for de Valera on cabinet committee and Skinner, *op. cit.*, pp. 72ff. on Lemass as post-war planner.

23. Committee files in SPO S.13026A/B.

24. I am indebted to Ms McNamara of the Oireachtas Library for this reference from Riar na hOibre.

25. Covering note by MacEntee, 24 Sept. 1940, to a letter from Rev. Lewis Watt S.J. in *The Tablet*, requesting it be

[136] drawn to attention of members of government, SPO S.11265A. Memorandum below in SPO S.13053.

26. See de Valera's position on extending the powers of the Central Bank in M. Moynihan, *Currency and Central Banking*, p. 289.

27. PDDE 90/576, 26 May 1943; introduced 20 May, Lemass quotation at 90/472.

28. PDDE 91/220-21, 2 July 1943. References to committee meetings in SPO S.13026A as under: agriculture and land purchase 3 Mar.; education 14 Apr., 12 May; shipping, posts and mineral development 6 Oct.; Archbishop of Dublin 13 Dec.

29. He secured agreement to a Seanad amendment on the former and was granted leave to introduce the latter on 16 Feb. 1944, PDDE 92/1132-3.

30. PDDE 93/2430-31, 9 May 1944. Regarding rumours within Fianna Fáil, one informed source has reported a cabinet colleague referring to Lemass as 'that crook' and recalls de Valera lashing a closed party convention for repeating rumours about Lemass. Cf. Andrews, 'At one point in his career he was victim of a slander campaign which through its very lack of truth and common decency, hurt him deeply', obituary in *Irish Press*, 12 May 1971. Another source confirmed this but reported that he did take one thing from the Minister's office — the first bar run off at Haulbowline after the establishment of Irish Steel, a typically tangible symbol of one of his achievements.

31. PDDE 93/1785ff., 2 May 1944. Lemass also insisted that 'the railways remain the backbone of our transport system' (col. 1976), thus maintaining his consistent identification with the interests of railway workers in his own constituency. Cf. speeches by him to meetings of railwaymen in Inchicore, as reported in the *Irish Press*, 14 Jan. 1933, 2 Feb. 1936, 17 June 1943, 23 May 1944. These references derived from Declan O'Connell, 'Political Sociology in Ireland', unpublished MA thesis, Department of Politics, UCD 1980.

32. *Report of Commission on Vocational Organisation*, section 349, p. 208. For a discussion on the controversy and the newspaper quotations below following this report, see J. Whyte, *Church and State in Modern Ireland 1923-1979*, Gill and Macmillan 1980, chapter IV, 'The issue takes shape: vocationalism versus bureaucracy, 1944-46'. Cf. Lee's comment that Lemass 'engaged in a wrangle, as

undignified as it was unworthy', J. Lee, 'Seán Lemass' in J. Lee ed., *Ireland 1945–70*, Gill and Macmillan 1979, [137] p. 21.

33. SPO S.13026B, thirty-sixth meeting, 13 July 1944. This reference also for Lemass quote below.
34. PDDE 94/431, 14 June 1944.
35. Quoted in Skinner, *op. cit.*, p. 75.
36. M. Viney, 'Kenneth Whitaker: power with glory', *Irish Times*, 2 May 1973.
37. File of departmental conferences, new series, 30 Aug. 1945-23 July 1948 in the Department of Industry and Commerce.
38. A carefully documented account of this relationship on which the following account is based, is contained in the definitive C. McCarthy, *Trade Unions in Ireland 1894-1960*, IPA Dublin 1977. Cf. D. Nevin, 'Industry and Labour' in K. B. Nowlan & T. D. Williams eds, *Ireland in the War Years and After, 1939-51*, Gill and Macmillan 1969, pp. 106-7. PDDE 88/1677, 29 Oct. 1942.
39. PDDE 101/1006, 1009, 28 May 1946.
40. Weekly conference, 1 Nov. 1945, Department of Industry and Commerce. Quotation below from weekly conference, 17 Dec. 1945. Dáil speech, PDDE 105/805-6, 17 Apr. 1947.
41. See Whitaker, *op. cit.*, pp. 414-15. Cf. Seán Lemass speech at Kilkenny in *Annual Register* 1947. The reference to a divergence with de Valera derived from interview with author.
42. E.g. a departmental conference noted permission to bring four French hat designers to a Galway hat factory 'subject to the character etc. of actual choices being in order' (22 Oct. 1945); an official was detailed to 'sound out' the proprietor of a new factory as to whether there was likely to be 'an alien infiltration of an undesirable kind' (25 Oct. 1945); in the case of admitting forty aliens to the Beltex Spinning Mills 'it was confirmed that the aliens would not be Jews and that the capital backing would not come from Jewish sources' (1 Nov. 1945).
43. Interview with the author. Cf. *Irish Weekly Independent*, 20 Dec. 1947, election meeting at Aughrim; and *Irish Press*, 10 Jan. 1948, Dublin cumann meeting.
44. *Irish Weekly Independent*, 31 Jan. 1948.

5: The Leader in Waiting (pp. 80-97)

1. These paragraphs based on interviews with Seán Lemass

and with members of the Lemass family. Cf. political correspondent's view that the National Labour group and about four independents would vote for de Valera and three or four abstain, *Irish Weekly Independent*, 31 Jan. 1948.

2. *Irish Times*, 10 Apr. 1948.

3. All references are to PDDE vol. 110; nomination of government, cols 49-66, 18 Feb.; vote on account, cols 223ff., 9 Mar.; Budget, cols 1058ff., 4 May; and vol. 112: Taoiseach's estimate, cols 1348ff., 22 July; Industry and Commerce, 1114ff., 21 July; Anglo-Irish Trade Agreement, cols 2167ff., 5 Aug. 1948.

4. For details see PDDE vols 110, 111 *passim*.

5. See *Irish Press*, 23 Feb. 1948; PDDE 110, cols 184 and 319ff., 9 Mar. 1948; speeches by Morrissey in Cloughjordan and Thurles in *Irish Weekly Independent*, 15 May and 13 Nov. 1948.

6. This information supplied by officials involved. For Leydon's view, see Roche, *op. cit.*, 242. For Lemass's attacks below see PDDE 114/1786ff., 29 Mar. 1948, vote on account; PDDE 115/2036, 25 May 1948, Industry and Commerce estimate.

7. PDDE 119/1595, 9 Mar. 1950. 2nd stage Industrial Development Bill, cf. col. 1857, 14 Mar. 1950. Supplementary estimate Industry and Commerce.

8. PDDE 126/1514ff., 12 July 1951, Industry and Commerce estimate.

9. PDDE 123/671ff., 764ff., 909ff. The reference to Liam Cosgrave from PDDE 126/1672, 17 July 1951, Industry and Commerce estimate debate. Information on Lemass's view below supplied by a senior civil servant. Morrissey subsequently challenged Lemass's volte-face on the Prices Advisory Body in his speech on the second stage of the Supplies and Services Bill 1952. PDDE 135, 177, 27 Nov. 1952.

10. PDDE 113/448ff. and 478ff., 24-5 Nov. 1948. Information on private view from interview with the author. Cf. *Nusight* profile, p. 88.

11. This section based on interviews with Mr Lemass and with party officials and members. Cf. B. Farrell, *Chairman or Chief?*, p. 56. For de Valera's ard fheis intervention see *Irish Weekly Independent*, 26 June 1948.

12. Longford-O'Neill, *Eamon de Valera*, p. 439.

13. PDDE 126/1502ff., 12 July 1951.

14. **PDDE** 126, 14 June 1951, e.g., Seán Dunne called him 'possibly one of the most able men in the House' (col. [139] 143); Oliver Flanagan, in a back-handed compliment, said, 'No matter what else may be said about him he is capable, he is efficient and he has plenty of brains' (col. 152).

15. The following account based on Moynihan, *op. cit.*, chap. 17; Fanning, *op. cit.*, pp. 468ff.; and PDDE vol. 127, *passim*.

16. **PDDE** 128/577.

17. This account based on interviews with Mr Lemass, officials and businessmen and PDDE, vols 134 and 136 *passim*.

18. **PDDE** 142/802, 28 Oct. 1953.

19. **PDDE** 135/890, 4 Dec. 1952, reply to second stage, Supplies and Services Bill 1952.

20. **PDDE** 142/98, 28 Oct. 1953.

21. The following account derived from Fanning, *op. cit.*, 'The Cabinet Committee on the Provision of Employment', pp. 495-500.

22. **PDDE** 140/349-50, 1 July 1953, vote of confidence motion.

23. Extracts from internal records supplied by Fianna Fáil. Information on the reorganisation from members of the group and Mr Joe O'Neill.

24. Quotation from M. Mills, *op. cit.*, 31 Jan. 1969. Cf. *Irish Press*, 23 Nov. 1955.

25. Profile (by P. Lynch) of Lemass in *The Leader*, 13 Mar. 1954. On Clery's Ballroom speech below, see *Irish Press*, 11 Oct. 1955.

26. T. K. Whitaker, *op. cit.*, p. 416.

27. Reported in *Irish Press* lead story, 9 Nov. 1955.

28. *Irish Press*, 18 Jan. 1957. For 'interview' below, see *Sunday Press*, 27 Jan. 1957. The last sentence was quoted at the top of the story. A footnote added, 'there are now 94,585 people unemployed compared with 70,465 this time last year.'

29. Interview with Mr Lemass. Subsequent paragraph derived from interviews as indicated in B. Farrell, *Chairman or Chief? the role of Taoiseach in Irish Government*, Gill and Macmillan, Dublin 1971.

30. Whitaker, *op. cit.*, p.416.

31. *Irish Press*, 29 Oct. 1958.

32. James Meenan, 'The Republic of Ireland', in *Annual Register* 1958, p. 281.

[140]

33. *Irish Press*, 25 Apr. 1959. This and subsequent paragraph based on discussion with Mr Lemass on draft of chapter 5, *Chairman or Chief?* and on interview with senior official.

Chapter 6: Lemass as Taoiseach (pp. 98-124)
Much of the material in this chapter is based on information supplied for Chapter 5 of *Chairman or Chief?* and is sometimes covered more fully there.

1. PDDE 176/140 and 139ff., 23 June 1959.
2. The references in the following two paragraphs are: Fianna Fáil meeting, Cruise's Hotel, Limerick, 5 Dec. 1959; interview with H. Carr, *Guardian*, 27 Apr. 1960; Muintir na Tíre, Rockwell College, 19 Aug. 1960; Budget speech, PDDE 181/458, 3 May 1960; Dublin Chamber of Commerce, 25 Oct. 1960; final comment in James Meenan, 'Republic of Ireland' in *Annual Register* 1959, p. 284.
3. The references are to PDDE 176/1-86, 23 June 1959.
4. I am indebted to Séamus Puirséil for drawing my attention to this point and to the Industry and Commerce background of Bartley and Hilliard noted below.
5. PDDE 176/91, 23 June 1959.
6. Information supplied by Miss A. Ormonde. Cf. debate on the nomination of government. All but one of the seven deputies who spoke regretted Deputy Ormonde's retirement through ill-health.
7. PDDE 176/1910-11, 23 July 1959.
8. PDDE 176/110-11, 23 June 1959. Lemass reference below at cols 136-7.
9. Information supplied by Mr Lemass and ministers involved.
10. On the Smith resignation, see Farrell *Chairman or Chief?*, pp. 65-7.
11. PDDE 212/93, 3 Nov. 1964.
12. PDDE 215/21, 21 Apr. 1965. Four of the six (Flanagan, Gibbons, Faulkner and Lalor) became ministers before the end of the decade.
13. M. Mills, *op. cit.*, 3 Feb. 1969.
14. Information on these two issues from personal interviews. For Lemass's response in the Dáil see PDDE 193/4ff., 14 Feb. 1962. For the evasion see his response to Norton at col. 9. Senator Eoin Ryan represented Fianna Fáil when the matter was discussed on RTE's magazine programme *Broadsheet*. On the O'Malley case below see Farrell, *op. cit.*, pp. 68-70.

15. M. Mills, *op. cit.*, 3 Feb. 1969. Quote below from ard fheis speech 10 Nov. 1959. Cf. PDDE 213/1302, 16 Dec. 1964, 'I regard it as my duty as head of the government to encourage argument at cabinet meetings: this is the way we get to see every side of the question.' [141]

16. The comments in this paragraph are all based on interviews with former ministerial and party colleagues.

17. 'Lemass on Government', an interview in *Léargas*, IPA, Dublin, no. 12, January 1968, p.3. Cf. the conclusion of his first speech on the estimate for the Department of the Taoiseach: 'I have changed within the month from the position in which it was my duty to know everything about something to one in which it is my duty, as I conceive it, to know something about everything, and I do not claim to be fully qualified yet. I hope that will excuse any shortcomings in the statement I have just made.' PDDE 176/1578, 21 July 1959.

18. PDDE 178/1541, adjournment debate, 11 Dec. 1959.

19. On the CIO and adaptation to free trade see G. FitzGerald, *Planning in Ireland*, IPA, Dublin 1968, pp. 57ff. Quote below in PDDE 175/938, 3 June 1959.

20. John Sheehan, 'Education and Society in Ireland, 1945-70' in J. Lee ed., *Ireland 1945-70*. Cf. Brown, *Ireland*, pp. 247ff.

21. PDDE 224/1046, reply to parliamentary question, 12 Oct. 1966. For a discussion see B. Farrell, 'The Mass Media and the 1977 Campaign' in H. Penniman ed., *Ireland at the Polls: the Dáil elections of 1977*, AEI Washington 1978, pp. 105ff. Cf. D. Fisher, *Broadcasting in Ireland*, Routledge and Kegan Paul, London 1978, pp. 31-3.

22. F. Sherwin, TD, PDDE 176/31, 23 June 1959. Quotation below from S. MacEntee, Lemass obituary in *Irish Press*, 12 May 1971.

23. File on 'Secretary's Discussions Abroad', Department of Industry and Commerce meeting in the Ministry of Fuel and Power, London, 21 Mar. 1947.

24. Speech to National Press Club, Washington. *Irish Press*, 2 Oct. 1953. The NATO hint to Ottawa Canadian Club, *Irish Press*, 'Border must go', 26 Feb. 1953.

25. PDDE 176/140, 23 June 1959. Cf. his remarks in M. Mills, *op. cit.*, 28 Jan. 1969: 'I would be appalled at the prospect for Ireland if the opportunity ever presented itself to us of bringing partition to an end by force, of compelling these people in the North who are now opposed to us

against their will. This would lead to a very dangerous situation which would require us to continue to exert force, and to repress hostility in the North. It would mean the creation, virtually, of a police state in the North. This would, I think, be detrimental to both North and South and morally destructive.' EFTA speech in Belfast to the Irish Association for Cultural, Social and Economic Relations, *Irish Press*, 11 Feb. 1958.

26. Lemass's reply to a parliamentary question on partition issue at UN: 'to raise the issue of partition at the United Nations at an inopportune time or on an inappropriate occasion would be likely to do more harm than good', PDDE 176/588, 7 July 1959. Cf. similar response to PQ PDDE 178/28ff., 18 Nov. 1959, 192/1242ff., 6 Dec. 1961. On terminology to describe the North an evasive reply to parliamentary questions, PDDE 183/1-4, 21 June 1960. On neutrality see P. Keatinge, *The Formulation of Irish Foreign Policy*, IPA Dublin 1973; cf. PDDE 197/12ff., 30 Oct. 1962. Other references in this paragraph: *Belfast Telegraph*, 9 July 1959; *Irish Press*, 24 Oct. 1959; *One Nation*, published by Fianna Fáil, n.d., speech to Oxford Union Society, 15 Oct. 1959.

27. PDDE 184/917, 10 Nov. 1960. The 1923 IRA order is referred to at col. 918. Quotation below in speech to Dublin South Central Fianna Fáil, *Irish Times*, 13 May 1961.

28. Interview with David Watt, political correspondent of *The Scotsman*, reported in *Irish Press*, 13 Feb. 1961. Television interview reported in *Irish Press*, 5 Aug. 1961. It was a point he emphasised frequently; cf. ard fheis speech, *Irish Press*, 17 Jan. 1962.

29. PDDE 201/113, 4 Apr. 1963. Earlier quotation at col. 736, 2 Apr. 1963. Cf. Terence O'Neill, *Autobiography*, Hart-Davis 1972, chap. VIII. The following account is based on this, part 8 of the Mills interview, *Irish Press*, 28 Jan. 1969, and interviews with a number of participants.

30. *Irish Times*, 12 May 1971.

31. Cf. Keatinge, *op. cit.*, pp. 60 and 93. Quotations below: PDDE 192/125, nomination of government, 11 Oct. 1961; Keatinge, *op. cit.*, p.70.

32. This account of the Congo decision is developed from that in *Chairman or Chief?* following final interview with Mr Lemass. For legislation see PDDE 183/1875-1905, Defence (Amendment) Bill 1960, 20 July 1960.

33. Cf. J. Lee, *op. cit.*, and T. Brown, *op. cit.* and the revision-ist critique by P. Bew and H. Patterson, *Seán Lemass and the Making of Modern Ireland 1945-66*, Gill and Macmillan, Dublin 1982. [143]

34. PDDE 191/2564, adjournment debate, 2 Aug. 1961. On the previous day he had formally announced Ireland's application for membership of the EEC, cols 2246ff.

35. He repeatedly stressed that he regarded the scheme of compulsory binding arbitration as a second-best to an agreed solution. For details see PDDE 191/2851-2986, Electricity (Temporary Provisions) Bill 1961, 1 Sept. 1961.

36. Reproduced in Farrell, *Chairman or Chief?*, pp. 66-7.

37. MacEntee, Lemass obituary, *Irish Press*, 12 May 1971.

38. For Lemass's speech see PDDE 200/102ff., 20 Feb. 1963. For his Budget contribution see PDDE 202/305, 24 Apr. 1963.

39. A series of reports in the *Irish Press* record him as joining the boards of Ryans, North and Co.; McDonagh & Boland (22 Nov. 1966); Ronald Lyon Estates (2 Dec. 1966); Electrical Industries of Ireland (7 Dec. 1966); Bateman Catering (9 Jan. 1967); he became chairman of Irish Security Services (12 May 1968) and of Unidare (24 Oct. 1968).

40. S. MacEntee, *op. cit.*

Index

National Development Fund (1954), 88
National Labour, 79, 80
National League, 19, 20
National Union of Journalists, 106
national wage agreement (1964), 121
neutrality, 64, 83
Norman, Mrs Mary Anne, 1
North Atlantic Treaty Organisation (NATO), 114

O'Brien, Paddy, 7
O'Connell, T. J., 24
O'Connor, Rory, 7
O'Dea, Jimmy, 4
O'Dea, Ken, 4
O'Doherty, Liam, 21
O'Donnell, Peadar, 20
O'Higgins, Kevin, 20
O'Higgins, M. J., 100
O'Higgins, T., 55
Oil and Fats Ltd, 60
O'Kelly, Seán T., 37, 53, 64, 67, 75
O'Malley, Donagh, 103, 106, 112
O'Malley, Ernie, 7
O'Neill, Joe, 89
O'Neill, Terence, 112, 116-17
O'Neill, T. P., 18
O'Reilly, M. W., 5
Ormonde, Seán, 102
Ottawa Conference (1932), 37

Pearse, Patrick, 5, 14
Pearse, Willie, 5
Poor Relief (Dublin) Bill (1929), 28
Prices Advisory Body, 83, 85
protection, 26
Public Safety Act (1927), 22

Radio Telefis Éireann (RTE), 112
Road Transport Advisory Board, 75, 76
Rooney, William, 2
Roosevelt, F. D., 30
Ruttledge, P. J., 15, 16, 54, 62, 65
Ryan, Eoin, 90
Ryan, James, 37, 47, 54, 60-61, 64, 73, 101, 102, 105, 118, 122

Saor Éire, 30
Shannon Free Airport Development Co., 77
Sinn Féin, 9, 12-20 *passim*, 25, 27, 32, 60, 61
Skinner, Liam, 5, 33
Smith, Patrick, 104, 121
Special Branch, 22
Stalin, Joseph, 30
Sunday Press, The, 80, 94
Supplies, Dept. of, 51, 53, 56, 58, 63, 65

Tariff Commission, 26
Tea Importers Ltd, 60
Timber Importers Ltd, 60
Tone, T. W., 14
Trade Union Act (1941), 76
Transport Act (1944), 70
Traynor, Oscar, 54, 103
Truman, Harry S., 39
turnover tax, 122

unemployment protests (1950s), 89
United Nations, 114, 118

Volunteers, 3-5. *See also* Irish Republican Army (IRA)

Whitaker, T. K., 93, 116